Recovery

Exercises

For Christians

Book One

Ken Gross

This page intentionally left blank.

Recovery Exercises for Christians

Book One

50 Written Exercises

Based on Scriptural Principles

Using an Assortment of Scriptures

Thank you Kathy Trout, my friend, co-worker in helping

others and editor of this book.

Notice – This book of written exercises is designed to be used by those in some form of recovery program and under the guidance of a sponsor, mentor, coach or counselor. It is written with the understanding that the publisher and author are not engaged in rendering any form of professional services. The exercises provided in this book are meant to be used by an individual or a group for study purposes, and they are not in any way designed to be a substitute for one-to-one professional therapy if such help is necessary.

About the Author

Ken was born in the UK, and at age three developed tuberculosis resulting in him being taken by his family to a sanitarium for treatment. This action of abandonment, although it saved his life, set him on a path that contained many struggles, and eventually led to recovery in his own life.

Before he got there, recovery, he obtained an undergraduate degree with a joint major in Chemistry and Physics from the University of London and an MBA from the University of Oklahoma. He spent some time working in the water industry in the UK, then the oil industry in Saudi Arabia and finally in the financial services industry here in the US.

In 2009 God gave him the vision for a new style of recovery ministry and he became the founding director of Merimnao (merimnao.org) which he still runs to this day. He also wrote and published three recovery oriented books, the "Emotional Prison" series. The three book series covers how emotions trap us; looks at the major emotional prisons that exist, such as religion, false intimacy and perfectionism; and how to become free of the prisons, or healed. These books are available through Merimnao or on amazon.com, including a kindle version.

Ken is available at director@merimnao.org for those that may wish to speak with him, request him to train group leaders in Christian recovery leadership or request him to speak at retreats.

Table of Contents

Recommendations

<u>For Sponsors, Mentors, Coaches, Pastors, Counselors or Other Spiritual Guides</u>

We recommend that those who are guiding others through recovery programs, a disciplined plan of spiritual formation, Christian lifestyle coaching or personal therapy use these exercises as an adjunct part of their work.

Every exercise is designed for the individual doing the work to provide written responses. They can be thought of as focused journaling, the writing down of specific thoughts and/or meditations relating to their personal plan of recovery or therapy in the context of God's word.

For 12 step program sponsors, although these exercises have a suggested step that the author believes might be appropriate, the sponsor can choose to use them as he or she sees fit. As such they help the sponsor to encourage their program participant look at a wide range of recovery topics more closely. We therefore suggest that the sponsee owns a personal copy of this book and the sponsor assigns exercises as appropriate, giving the sponsee time to complete one and coming back together to discuss the results and see what God may be revealing.

<u>For Program or Plan Participants</u>

These exercises are designed to assist and guide a personal introspection into an individual's heart, mind and will. This is always best done under the guidance of the Holy Spirit. This is why we suggest that before a person begins an exercise, they say a short prayer asking God through His Spirit to reveal what needs to be known or looked at in going through the work involved.

There is no right or wrong about any of the answers. The best results for a person doing this exercise come when they are open and honest with God, themselves and their program guide and give themselves time to do the work. Our experience suggests a minimum of a week per exercise.

General Instructions to Book Users

This is a workbook of sorts. While we have put in space for users to write in the book, the intent is for those doing the exercises to write their responses in other locations. Examples of this might be personal journals or recovery folders; something personal and private to an individual.

We do suggest that those assigning exercises write in the book of a program participant or other end user. Sometimes encouraging words can be added; or extra commentary on the scriptures being used or possibly more individualized direction and instructions. Each exercise has space allocated for this purpose.

Being thorough in doing the work, as in all work, yields the most optimal results for an individual using these exercises. Use the book with a view to being healed from something or overcoming a serious struggle. This is the kind of thing that the Apostle Paul was talking about in Philippians 2:12-13. As we adopt this attitude of working with an expectation of the Spirit doing something in us, the work becomes a part of our personal sanctification; which is God's saving work that He performs with us and in us throughout our lives.

You may notice that some of the exercises may be similar to one another; this is by design. Our experience in recovery work suggests that looking at the same problem from different perspectives is advantageous in achieving good program results. Included in each exercise is a short list of emotion and attitude words that could be used in an individual's written exercise response. At the back of the book, Addendum 3 contains a good selection of emotion/attitude words for reference.

Finally, we suggest that an individual keep all notes, answers and responses separate and private from other personal documentation as these exercises will reveal things to you that others may not understand and therefore misinterpret.

This page intentionally left blank.

Exercise 1

Romans 7:14-20

<u>Understanding Myself</u>

Rom 7:14-20 - For we know that the law is spiritual, but I am of the flesh, sold under sin. I do not understand my own actions. For I do not do what I want, but I do the very thing I hate. Now if I do what I do not want, I agree with the law, that it is good. So now it is no longer I who do it, but sin that dwells within me. For I know that nothing good dwells in me, that is, in my flesh. For I have the desire to do what is right, but not the ability to carry it out. For I do not do the good I want, but the evil I do not want is what I keep on doing. Now if I do what I do not want, it is no longer I who do it, but sin that dwells within me. ESV

<u>Guiding Commentary</u> - Paul, the man that wrote this under the guidance of the Holy Spirit, has been rightly called the world's greatest missionary and he wrote about two thirds of the entire New Testament. In this passage he expresses how much of a failure he was at trying to keep God's commands. He says he is constantly doing the things he doesn't want to and not doing the things he wants to. This is a confessional statement written for the benefit of all who read it. It has two elements that will be important to consider in your response, honesty before God and man, and truth about himself.

<u>The Exercise</u> – First, write out the scripture, and everywhere that you see the words "I" and "me" add in your first name next to it. (You can use your own preferred version of this scripture.)

Write out in essay form how this scripture describes you and your situation. Include details of moments when you have experienced thoughts and feelings that seem to fit with the sentiments of this set of verses. Try to identify words that express your emotions at those times and also how you feel about those past events today.

Sponsor Notes: _____

_____

_____

Useful Feeling Words:

- Powerless, Hopeless, Unworthy, Beaten, Defeated, Anger

Useful Attitudinal Words:

- Resentment, Bitterness, Hopelessness, Powerlessness

My Pre-exercise Notes: _____

_____

_____

_____

_____

The suggested step for Exercise 1 is Step 1.

Exercise 2

Romans 7:21-25

<u>Internal Conflict</u>

Rom 7:21-25 - So I find it to be a law that when I want to do right, evil lies close at hand. For I delight in the law of God, in my inner being, but I see in my members another law waging war against the law of my mind and making me captive to the law of sin that dwells in my members. Wretched man that I am! Who will deliver me from this body of death? Thanks be to God through Jesus Christ our Lord! So then, I myself serve the law of God with my mind, but with my flesh I serve the law of sin. ESV

<u>Guiding Commentary</u> - For context, it might also be wise to read the prior verses (14-20). In this set of verses, Paul examines the conflict inside of every believer; he calls it a war between the law of God and the law of sin. Another way of describing this is a war between our natural self and our regenerated spirit.

One helpful way to understand how we look, psychologically speaking, when we become a born again Christian is as follows. Prior to the moment of salvation our soul (inner man) was ruled totally by our self-oriented beliefs, values and attitudes. After salvation, we have given at least a small part of our inner man to Christ and that part is ruled by the Holy Spirit. As we mature in our Christian walk we give a bigger and bigger part of our inner man over to the rule and reign of Christ. So then, there is always a war between our self-centered nature and the part ruled over by God. As God can never lose this battle, we occasionally find ourselves in a miserable state of wanting or lusting for one thing, and God saying through the Holy Spirit in us, "No!" that is not good for my child. Paul uses the word "wretched" to describe this.

<u>The Exercise</u> – First, write out the scripture, and everywhere that you see the words "I" and "me" add in your first name next to it. (You can use your own preferred version of this scripture.)

Take some time to meditate on how this war has been played out in your life. Then, write out in essay form a detailed account of some of your experiences of these inner battles. In particular try to identify the struggle between acting under your own will and that of the Spirit.

This is likely to take some time to complete, and is going to be lengthy in its final form, maybe two or more pages long.

Sponsor Notes: _____

_____

_____

Useful Feeling Words:

- Desire, Compromised, Overtaken, Weak, Lust, Angry

Useful Attitudinal Words:

- Selfish, Negative, Ungrateful, Audacious, Contradictory

My Pre-exercise Notes: _____

_____

_____

_____

The suggested step for Exercise 2 is Step 3.

Exercise 3

Ephesians 6:16

How is Your Shield?

Eph 6:16 - In all circumstances take up the shield of faith, with which you can extinguish all the flaming darts of the evil one. ESV

<u>Guiding Commentary</u> – This is part of the instruction from the Apostle Paul about "putting on the armor of God" found in Ephesians 6:10-18. While each of the pieces of armor is important, this piece carries a special meaning for those of us in recovery.

Recovery, in large part, is a work we engage in to remove false beliefs from our heart and replace them with godly beliefs (truth). The reason we say this is because every human acts from their beliefs, values and attitudes. It is our ungodly beliefs that allow us to "act out" in some way, and sometimes these beliefs are buried so deep we aren't able to connect with what they are, even though the results of having them are apparent in our actions.

In this scripture we are encouraged, in an instructional way, to put up a shield of faith which will protect us from the messages of the enemy, the world and our self-centered nature. Faith is all about what we believe and it is the defensive weapon given to us by God to help us fend off attacks. Attacks for those of us in recovery seem to be mostly temptations, messages of worthlessness and a desire to isolate.

So how do we develop a shield of faith? God's word (Rom 10:17) says that faith comes by hearing the word of God. Developing a protecting faith then is done by going to church, listening to the Holy Spirit, Bible study and fellowshipping with those in Christian recovery.

<u>The Exercise</u> - Write out the story of two times you felt attacked. Make them as detailed as is reasonable. Include a description of the circumstances of the story, things like geography, people involved, what was going on in your life at that time. Spell out how you felt attacked, if you felt overwhelmed, if your belief in God was challenged and any other emotional conditions you can remember. Talk about how

8

you handled it, for example, did you ask for help, did you pray or pick up your Bible or did you just "suck it up" and hope it went away?

After writing these things out, scribble down your appraisal of how well you think your shield is prepared for the inevitable future attacks. Whatever its condition, what are you going to do to improve its efficacy?

Sponsor Notes: _____

_____

_____

Useful Feeling Words:

- Attacked, Powerless, Overtaken, Beaten, Defeated, Anger

Useful Attitudinal Words:

- Passive, Outraged, Bitterness, Hopelessness, Weakness

My Pre-exercise Notes: _____

_____

_____

_____

_____

The suggested step for Exercise 3 is Step 10.

Exercise 4

John 1:14

<u>Truth or Grace?</u>

John 1:14 - And the Word became flesh and dwelt among us, and we have seen his glory, glory as of the only Son from the Father, full of grace and truth. ESV

<u>Guiding Commentary</u> – This is part of John's introduction to his gospel where he familiarizes us with his personal friend, Jesus, who he knew intimately from having travelled around the Holy Land with Him for about 3 years. In this verse John says that Jesus (the Word) became a man and lived with us, and that He was full of grace and truth. This means that he was full of both grace and truth!

So often we are told to be balanced about being truthful and grace-filled in our recovery, as if we have to give one up sometimes for the other. This idea of balance sometimes results in situations where when we attempt to help others we might be "truthful" but lack grace and seem as condemning or critical; or, we might also come across as "grace-filled" but not really address what needs to be said, and so almost say that unsound behaviors are acceptable.

Our aim ought to always be to deliver truth in a gracious way as we walk with others as sponsors, accountability partners, group facilitators or as simply friends in our fellowships. We ought to be aiming to "max out" in both positive attributes, just like Jesus did.

<u>The Exercise</u> - Think of a time in your early recovery when you were on the receiving end of some help and experienced an individual giving you a dose of truth, but in a less than grace-filled way. Write about it, describe the incident, but don't name the people. Make a discerning judgment as to what your helper was motivated by, and comment on it.

Now do the same for a time when you ought to have heard more truth, but got mostly grace and looking back you sense they maybe you were let off the hook over something. Write about it in the same way.

For the third part of this exercise, do the same for when you were trying to help others. Think of one time you were abundantly truthful, but a little short on the grace, and vice versa.

What does all this tell you about helping others in truth and grace? And what does it tell you about how you handle truth and grace personally.

Sponsor Notes: _____

_____

_____

Useful Feeling Words:

- Judged, Condemned, Attacked, Beaten, Anger

Useful Attitudinal Words:

- Rebelliousness, Outraged, Bitterness, Resentment

My Pre-exercise Notes: _____

_____

_____

_____

The suggested step for Exercise 4 is Step 12.

Exercise 5

Philippians 2:12-13

<u>Cleansing of the Heart</u>

Phil 2:12-13 - Therefore, my beloved, as you have always obeyed, so now, not only as in my presence but much more in my absence, work out your own salvation with fear and trembling, for it is God who works in you, both to will and to work for his good pleasure. **ESV**

<u>Guiding Commentary</u> – In this selected scripture we see that the Apostle Paul, under instruction from the Holy Spirit, is passing on God's command for us to work on ourselves. Paul uses the words "fear and trembling" to indicate we ought to have an attitude of reverence in our submission to God. He goes on to reassure us that God is working in us for His purposes, which will always be to our benefit and God's glory.

<u>The Exercise</u> - Look up the word "sanctification" in a Bible glossary or an on-line resource. Write down the definition. Now consider how you might be working on your own sanctification (which Paul calls "working out our salvation"). List some of the things you have been doing to "clean up your act" over the last year or two. As you do this, reflect and comment in writing if you see that God has been assisting you in this process of sanctification. Be specific about what part of your change or growth was due to you and what part was due to the Holy Spirit.

As far as you can, identify character defects that you have been able to overcome and also identify new godly character traits you have installed in your heart. How have these changes in the nature of your character improved your relationships? As far as you can, list improvements in marital, work and social (church) relationships.

Finally write out some of the things you would like God to help you "work out with fear and trembling" over the next couple of years. Include the reason(s) you want to work on these particular items. This will help a trusted advisor understand your motivations and commitment to yourself.

Sponsor Notes: _____

_____

_____

Useful Feeling Words:

- Clean, Dirty, Whole, Healed, Healthy

Useful Attitudinal Words:

- Thankful, Excited, Expectant, Joyful, Apprehensive

My Pre-exercise Notes: _____

_____

_____

_____

_____

The suggested step for Exercise 5 is Step 10.

Exercise 6

2 Corinthians 3:16-17

<u>Out of Captivity</u>

2 Cor 3:16-17 - But when one turns to the Lord, the veil is removed. Now the Lord is the Spirit, and where the Spirit of the Lord is, there is freedom. ESV

<u>Guiding Commentary</u> – This section of scripture talks about being bold in our Christian lives, in the sense of sharing the gospel, as we under a new covenant because of Jesus' sacrifice. This covenant includes the components that are shared by God with us in the two verses above. Whenever a person turns to the Lord, which is normally called the moment of salvation, the veil of their heart is taken away and the Holy Spirit enters their heart to begin the Christian life. Once we have the Spirit inside us we have the availability of freedom.

In recovery this has some importance. We have all been in slavery to something, in bondage to compulsive activity of some kind. It operated like an idol that was in charge of our lives, and for the most part we couldn't see what it was doing to us and those we love. Once God, in the form of the Holy Spirit enters us, the veil is lifted, meaning we can see the truth about ourselves more clearly. Then as the truth filters into our mind, heart and will, we become free; that is - up to a point!

That point is whatever we choose it to be. So many of us have a kind of 'Stockholm Syndrome" where we were kidnapped by an idol and identify with our captor and cannot break to complete freedom without help. In the context of recovery one of the big steps to freedom from our slavery and from the power of the idol is dealing with the problems inside of us. To do this we must humbly ask the Holy Spirit to help us remove our character defects.

<u>The Exercise</u> – In this exercise we are to write out a description of each of our major character defects. By this we mean give each defect a word name, and then define it in your own words much like a dictionary might. For example – Laziness – I am too apathetic to bother dealing with my problems.

Then write out a personal prayer to God humbly asking him to help you, through His Holy Spirit, to remove the character defects you listed in the first part of this exercise. Finally pray this prayer for yourself once a day for one week, and then discuss this exercise with your Christian spiritual guide.

Sponsor Notes: _____

_____

_____

Useful Feeling Words:

- Sorrow, Sadness, Hopeful, Transformed, Changed

Useful Attitudinal Words:

- Thankful, Regretful, Forgiven, Repentful, Apathetic

My Pre-exercise Notes: _____

_____

_____

_____

The suggested step for Exercise 6 is Step 6.

Exercise 7

James 5:16

Confession to One Another

James 5:16 - Therefore, confess your sins to one another and pray for one another, that you may be healed. The prayer of a righteous person has great power as it is working. ESV

<u>Guiding Commentary</u> – This is a familiar verse to those in recovery and it has many components to it. First we see that we are instructed to confess to <u>one another</u>: this highlights the relational nature of healing in recovery. We are to also pray for each other. This scripture takes these two things, confession to and prayer for others, and tells us that it puts us in a position to be healed, not that we *will* be healed, just that we are in a place where we *can* be healed. It then adds that the prayer of a righteous person has great power, other translations of scripture use the word effective. The word translated as "working" (or effective) is a derivative of the Greek word "energeo", meaning with energy, implying a deep fervency and sincerity of prayer.

<u>The Exercise</u> – In this exercise we are not going to look at our actual confessions, we are going to focus on the relational aspects of healing and look into ourselves.

Write out your thoughts and personal understanding of why God has instructed us to confess to others, as well as to him (1 Jn 1:9). Then explain why you believe God has commanded us to not only confess but also to pray for each other and then link these two things to healing.

Next write down what you understand by the terms "effective or working prayer" and "righteous person" (tip – read 1 Jn 1:9 again) in our selected verse.

Lastly, take a look at what you have actually done and honestly assess your progress in obeying this instruction. Have you willingly, openly and honestly confessed your sins, character flaws, weaknesses and so on to others? Have you listened as others have confessed to you or in your presence in a meeting, and then prayed for them as the Holy Spirit leads you? Have you been deep and sincere in your prayers for yourself and others? Do you consider it an honor and privilege or a chore and a waste of your time to hear the confession of others? Write a journal entry or something similar about how well you've done in the recent past in each of these things.

Sponsor Notes: _____

_____

_____

Useful Feeling Words:

- Glad, Comforted, Joy, Happy, Troubled, Sincere

Useful Attitudinal Words:

- Forgiven, Thankful, Fearful, Anxious, Reluctant

My Pre-exercise Notes: _____

_____

_____

_____

The suggested step for Exercise 7 is Step 5.

Exercise 8

1 John 1:8-10

<u>Confession to God</u>

1 John 1:8-10 - If we say we have no sin, we deceive ourselves, and the truth is not in us. If we confess our sins, he is faithful and just to forgive us our sins and to cleanse us from all unrighteousness. If we say we have not sinned, we make him a liar, and his word is not in us. ESV

<u>Guiding Commentary</u> – These verses address our relationship with the Lord Himself. It starts from a place those in recovery will recognize, the confrontation of denial. None of us can honestly deny our sin, our character defects, our compulsive behaviors and lustful thoughts. In verse nine, God speaks to us and tells us unequivocally that He stands ready to forgive us and cleanse us, all we have do is to confess to Him. Then comes a scary verse; if we say we haven't sinned or don't sin, we are calling God a liar, and His truth is not in us. Effectively this means we are going forward without Him to help us, we are saying NO to Him, "leave me alone I'll do things my way." Denial of the truth that we sin is a barrier to successful and healthy recovery.

<u>The Exercise</u> – Looking back, can you remember your denial? Write about the first time you can remember that you came out of denial about an issue. Talk about the circumstances and events that led up to your confession and breaking through of the barrier to healing that we call denial. Tell about how you felt that day, and then speak to how you felt after some time. Did God come through on His promise in verse nine to "cleanse you from all unrighteousness"?

Go through this process for each time you have realized that you have broken through some denial about something. It is suggested in the interests of brevity that you limit yourself to maybe a total of three denials that have been overcome.

As you write, feel free to add anything that comes to you that you believe is relevant to this piece of scripture or exercise. Different people have different responses to this set of verses and it is healing to write out whatever the Lord gives you here.

(Study tip – there are three major areas of denial, denial of facts (truth), denial of seriousness (minimization) and denial of responsibility (blame others). Use these in your written response to this exercise.)

Sponsor Notes: _____

_____

_____

Useful Feeling Words:

- Glad, Clean, Joy, Happy, Troubled, Sincere

Useful Attitudinal Words:

- Denial, Forgiven, Contemptuous, Anxious, Rebelliousness

My Pre-exercise Notes: _____

_____

_____

_____

_____

The suggested step for Exercise 8 is Step 5.

Exercise 9

Romans 12:1-2

<u>Transformation</u>

Rom 12:1-2 - I appeal to you therefore, brothers, by the mercies of God, to present your bodies as a living sacrifice, holy and acceptable to God, which is your spiritual worship. Do not be conformed to this world, but be transformed by the renewal of your mind, that by testing you may discern what is the will of God, what is good and acceptable and perfect. ESV

<u>Guiding Commentary</u> – In this well used passage, which is an excellent alternative description of how we are to see recovery, God is speaking clearly. He is instructing us through the words of the Apostle Paul to present ourselves fully and completely to Him, and to throw ourselves on His mercy. Then Paul connects the giving of our complete selves, a living sacrifice, with transformation. When we go through a God centered transformation we are going through recovery, and when we do this within God's care, we are glorifying Him. Paul calls it proving the good and acceptable perfect will of God.

<u>The Exercise</u> – Before starting this exercise, be sure to sit with your sponsor or other Christian guide and discuss with them their understanding of these verses in the context of their own recovery, and also ask for their guidance on what they expect to see from you. Ask them to write their answer on the next page.

Discuss how much or little you have given of yourself to God; put your answer in a historical context. That is, tell us how much you gave yourself in the early days of dealing with issues, and how much more (or not) you have later. Did you throw yourself onto the mercy of God, who is completely trustworthy? As you did this, did you begin to stop seeing things the same old way? What behaviors did you stop, what new choices did you make, and what do you see differently now? Have others commented on any "transformation" they have seen in you? Has anybody particularly noticed and spoken, unsolicited, about any level of increased godliness in your behaviors? Godliness is the virtue of being more like Christ in your character, which is demonstrated in your actions. Tell us how easy or hard some of your transforming has been.

Finally, tell us what you are currently working on, in the context of not conforming to this world, what worldly behaviors you are trying to shirk, and how it is going.

Sponsor Notes: _____

_____

_____

Useful Feeling Words:

- Changed, Saved, Glad, Clean, Joy, Happy, Shame, Guilt

Useful Attitudinal Words:

- Freedom, Honesty, Transformed, Restored, Reconciled

My Pre-exercise Notes: _____

_____

_____

_____

_____

The suggested step for Exercise 9 is Step 7.

Exercise 10

Mark 12:28-31

<u>Loving Oneself.</u>

Mark 12:28-32 - And one of the scribes came up and heard them disputing with one another, and seeing that he answered them well, asked him, "Which commandment is the most important of all?" Jesus answered, "The most important is, 'Hear, O Israel: The Lord our God, the Lord is one. And you shall love the Lord your God with all your heart and with all your soul and with all your mind and with all your strength.' The second is this: 'You shall love your neighbor as yourself.' There is no other commandment greater than these."
ESV

<u>Guiding Commentary</u> – This is a well-recognized scripture, where Jesus is answering the question about which commandment is greatest. Our focus here is on the second greatest commandment, which Jesus was not asked about. It is to "love your neighbor as yourself". For those of us in Christian recovery, the very last part of this is an important command to know, understand and appreciate. We are instructed by the one who created us to "love ourselves".

<u>The Exercise</u> – There seems to be two ways we tend to "love ourselves", one is narcissistic, the other godly. Look up the term "narcissistic", and if you are so inclined find and read a copy of the story of Narcissus from Greek mythology, after whom the term "narcissistic" is named.

Now write down how you have historically thought and felt about yourself, or put another way, how you have loved yourself. Also record some of the major character defects that you found in yourself. Then record the outcomes of your acting out on you and the people around you. Were you narcissistic to any extent? Was your life "all about you?"

Read 1 Cor 13:4-8 and see if you have moved away from unhealthy self love (narcissism) to more healthy or godly form of self love by comparing this list of attributes of love with your current character. Record how much progress you have made in this and how you feel about it so far. Do you believe you must love yourself, or do you sense that this might not be a true Christian value?

Lastly, write down what effect loving yourself in a godly way might have on your own sense of self worth and how others perceive you. Also, record your expectation about what might happen in your relationships with others, particularly your nuclear family, if you had a healthy self-love.

Sponsor Notes: _____

_____

_____

Useful Feeling Words:

- Selfish, Affirmed, Admired, Cherished, Appreciated

Useful Attitudinal Words:

- Open, Honest, Receptive, Self-centered, Self-respect

My Pre-exercise Notes: _____

_____

_____

_____

_____

The suggested step for Exercise 10 is Step 4.

Exercise 11

2 Corinthians 1:3-4

<u>Comforting Others</u>

2 Cor 1:3-4 - Blessed be the God and Father of our Lord Jesus Christ, the Father of mercies and God of all comfort, who comforts us in all our affliction, so that we may be able to comfort those who are in any affliction, with the comfort with which we ourselves are comforted by God. ESV

<u>Guiding Commentary</u> – This is one of those very long sentences we sometimes find in the scriptures that is broken into two verses, and most likely should not have been, because it is one continuous thought from God. It starts with a word of thanks to God, and names Him as the Father of mercies, and the God of all comfort. It continues by stating that he has "been there" for us as He comforts us in all our afflictions. Then this scripture says something very important for those in recovery to absorb. God says we are enabled, through His comforting of us, to go and comfort others in their afflictions. Under the power and guidance of the Holy Spirit we are to "be there" for others who are experiencing troubles.

<u>The Exercise</u> – Think back to times when you were suffering an affliction, whether you were the cause of it or not. Name, by writing their actual names out, all the people that God sent to comfort you in your times of trouble. Go deep with this moment of thankfulness, name all those who directly gave you assistance, and all those that helped you but were not visible to you. (For example, if one person helped you in person, their spouse also helped; another example is where a preacher or teacher said something that comforted you. Also remember that God can send non-Christians to help too!) Organize it into situations or times of trouble in some way, and link the names for your sponsor or mentor to be able to connect the dots of your life. Comment on whether God sent these people into your life or not. As you complete this part, say a short prayer of thanks to God for these people.

In the second part, name the people you have "been there" for, even if they went back into their troubles or simply didn't listen to your counsel. Name them, and list their circumstances, and what you actually did. Comment also on whether you believe that God put you in those situations to help or if it was just a chance encounter. Speak about how you felt if your help was accepted, or if it was rejected, and if you felt responsible for whatever choices they made after your help.

Lastly, talk about how being comforted and comforting others has changed you. Talk particularly about how it has changed your beliefs, values and attitudes.

Sponsor Notes: _____

_____

_____

Useful Feeling Words:

- Selfish, Affirmed, Admired, Cherished, Appreciated

Useful Attitudinal Words:

- Open, Honest, Receptive, Self-centered, Self-respect

My Pre-exercise Notes: _____

_____

_____

_____

_____

The suggested step for Exercise 11 is Step 12.

Exercise 12

Colossians 2:8

Don't Be Fooled

Col 2:8 - See to it that no one takes you captive by philosophy and empty deceit, according to human tradition, according to the elemental spirits of the world, and not according to Christ. ESV

Guiding Commentary – This scripture is a global warning of the danger of listening, and paying attention to, the messages that the world delivers to us. Simple examples of this are the ads that urge us to buy the new car, or ask our doctor about the latest drug treatment for something (hollow and deceptive philosophies). Other more sophisticated examples are the pressure put on us by our family of origin or the church we were brought up in, which the writer of this verse calls "human tradition." The most important part of the warning for us in Christian recovery is what God calls here, "elemental spiritual forces."

Christian recovery faces a daily onslaught of messages from the recovery practitioners (for example unbelieving counselors and secular 12 step groups) who operate in the world and with worldly viewpoints. While they may be entirely sincere and seem knowledgeable, their allegiance is to the god of this world, even though they may not realize it. They effectively become the hands, feet and mouth of the enemy; and our scripture calls them elemental spiritual forces.

This means that those of us in Christian recovery must always have our guard up against the forces of secular recovery that attempt to lead us astray. Some of the common ways this happens are through temptations to take an easy path, to think that once we are sober, we are healed or that a few sessions with a counselor is all we need.

The Exercise – This exercise is merely meant for us to develop a healthy respect for the truth of our focus verse and to help us emphasize caution in whom and what we listen to in our Christ-centered recovery work. For this reason we don't need to identify the people involved in the stories we are asking you to write here.

Take a look back in your efforts to work on your issues, even going back to when you had not committed to Christian recovery. Write out a short description of each significant occurrence of being given a message that you now know was not a godly message. For example you may have been told to "just pray about it" or to "white knuckle it" or "to take pills for it" or to "see a psychic healer" or go to a secular psychiatrist/psychologist. Even well-meaning Christians may have delivered messages based on erroneous application of scriptures.

Sponsor Notes: _____

_____

_____

Useful Feeling Words:

- Hoodwinked, Deceived, Blind, Upset, Humbled

Useful Attitudinal Words:

- Humility, Honesty, Dark-minded, Freed, Released

My Pre-exercise Notes: _____

_____

_____

_____

_____

The suggested step for Exercise 12 is Step 3.

Exercise 13

Lamentations 3:40

Looking Inside

Lam 3:40-41 - Let us test and examine our ways, and return to the Lord! Let us lift up our hearts and hands to God in heaven. ESV

Guiding Commentary – This piece of the Lamentations of the prophet Jeremiah speaks to our internal motivations in looking for healing and relief from the compulsions that bind us. Are we willing to really look inside, no matter what may be in there? Are we going to truly examine and probe or test our thoughts, feelings, willful decisions and behaviors in rigorous honesty? The answer to this is that none of us will actually do this within our own power. The second verse here tells us how to actually become fearless about examining ourselves. We must lift up our heart and hands toward God; we must expose our soul, our everything to Him. He can be trusted to help reveal our character defects, our weaknesses and our issues to us without leaving us feeling punished by the shame and guilt we all carry. As we work on getting to the bottom of our troubles, we can slowly become unafraid of confessing our "stuff". This is because as we have trusted God, He has enabled us to conquer our fears through the support and comfort of the Holy Spirit.

The Exercise – In this exercise we will look at the process of searching inside our souls. If you have ever done some kind of spiritual or moral inventory, write about how the process unfolded for you. Talk about your fears, talk about your procrastination, talk about your avoidance of completing the task. Were you afraid that God would force you to look in places you didn't want to go? Did you have to go through the exercise more than once? If so, why was that? How do you feel about the inventory now? Would you like to go through it and be more thorough, and do you have a desire to have more of your "stuff" exposed by God?

If you are yet to go through an inventory process, are you dreading it? Talk about your fears; help a sponsor or mentor understand where you are emotionally in dealing with your issues by writing out your feelings about looking deep inside. Do you think you will engage in avoiding doing the work? Do you think you might run from God, instead of going toward Him with heart and hands open as our scripture instructs us? Are you ready to get your troubles looked at in detail?

What barriers to completing a spiritual or moral inventory do you anticipate putting up or otherwise experiencing? Are there people in your life that will either help or hinder your progress in developing your inventory? Be sure to identify them by name in your answer?

Sponsor Notes: _____

_____

_____

Useful Feeling Words:

- Afraid, Tense, Nervous, Anxious, Concerned

Useful Attitudinal Words:

- Procrastinate, Prideful, Grateful, Melancholy, Serious

My Pre-exercise Notes: _____

_____

_____

_____

_____

The suggested step for Exercise 13 is Step 4.

Exercise 14

1 Samuel 15:22-23(a)

Obedience or Rebellion

1 Sam 15:22-23(a) - And Samuel said, "Has the Lord as great delight in burnt offerings and sacrifices, as in obeying the voice of the Lord? Behold, to obey is better than sacrifice, and to listen than the fat of rams. For rebellion is as the sin of divination, and presumption is as iniquity and idolatry. ESV

Guiding Commentary – In this piece of scripture we see the anointed prophet of God, Samuel, speaking words of great wisdom under the direction of the Holy Spirit. While the Lord "delights" in our offerings and sacrifices, He would much rather have our obedience and that we would listen, meaning hear and do what He says, than receive what he calls "the fat of rams" which represents the best natural sacrificial offering we could possibly give Him. The scripture goes on to say that rebellion is as bad as divination (witchcraft) and insubordination (presumption) is as bad as deep sin (iniquity) and idol worship. Strong words indeed!

The Exercise – In this exercise we are going to look at our obedience to God and rebellion against Him. In the context of this exercise, obedience is voluntarily choosing to do what God says, and rebellion is knowingly doing our will and not His will.

Write a summary of how you rebelled against the will of God before you entered recovery. In doing this, give at least three examples of areas of rebellion in your life, comparing them to what you know God's word says. (An example may be that you drank too much, and God says don't get drunk.) Then move on to talk about any areas of disobedience that you struggled with as you were actually working your program, but believe that you may have now overcome. Finally talk about the areas that you know you are continuing to struggle with; parts of your life where you continue to be rebellious. Be specific and detailed, but not long-winded in this.

The last part of this exercise involves your thought life. Are you continuing to have thoughts cross your mind that indicate rebelliousness? Do you indulge in wishful thinking or fantasizing about being able to act out as you used to? Are you really giving up these things to God through prayer and meditation? Is obedience to God a real heart's desire of yours? Be as honest as you know how in these answers as it will help your sponsor or mentor to understand your daily struggles in a way that they will be able to more proficiently assist you.

Sponsor Notes: _____

_____

_____

Useful Feeling Words:

- Uncomfortable , Concerned, Afraid, Ashamed, Guilty

Useful Attitudinal Words:

- Rebellious, Obstinate, Prideful, Ignorant, Hard-hearted, Evasive

My Pre-exercise Notes: _____

_____

_____

_____

_____

The suggested step for Exercise 14 is Step 11.

Exercise 15

Luke 14:11

Humility is Necessary

Luke 14:11 - For everyone who exalts himself will be humbled, and he who humbles himself will be exalted. ESV

Guiding Commentary – This verse contains words that Jesus spoke directly to us. There should be no doubt in the mind of a reader of this verse about what Jesus is saying. People who are prideful will be humbled, and people who live in humility will be lifted up. Jesus doesn't tell us when the humbling or the lifting up will happen, just that it will. He is asking us here to voluntarily place ourselves under His care, humbling ourselves before Him and others. His promise is that if we do that He will lift us up. For those in recovery this is an important and urgent message. We have brought ourselves to low points in life; we have been humbled, through our own choices, made under our own wills. The message here is to go forward with a different mindset; we are to place ourselves with a sincere and humble heart, under the care of Jesus. His promise to us if we do this is to lift us up; this means He will renew us, restore us and enable reconciliation of some important relationships in our lives. It all begins with our humility.

The Exercise – Pride is a significant barrier to recovery. Talk about the way pride has colored your life before recovery. Discuss the areas of your life that displayed pride. Examples might be pride of performance, pride in how you dressed, pride in your possessions, and pride in how much you earn. Talk then about how pride has hurt you, how it was a contributing factor in you getting into your compulsions or addictions, and also in staying there.

Now move on to how pride might be affecting you today. Are you still proud of the things you discussed already? Are you too proud to accept that you are a detestable sinner? Are you too proud to reach out for help? Are you too proud to accept the truth about your character defects and weaknesses?

Finally, are you ready to accept the bad news about yourself and go to God in humility? When you really are ready, God is willing and able to lift you up. Do you believe God enough to humble yourself? If you are ready, write out a prayer of submission to God in genuine humility asking Him to help you see your shortcomings the way He does. As you do this, be sure to remember that God is never fooled by false humility.

Sponsor Notes: _____

_____

_____

Useful Feeling Words:

- Prideful, Self-important, Ashamed, Humiliated, Vulnerable

Useful Attitudinal Words:

- Prideful, Selfish, Narcissistic, Rebellious, Obstinate

My Pre-exercise Notes: _____

_____

_____

_____

_____

The suggested step for Exercise 15 is Step 6.

Exercise 16

Ephesians 4:25

Speaking Truth

Eph 4:25 - Therefore, having put away falsehood, let each one of you speak the truth with his neighbor, for we are members one of another. ESV

Guiding Commentary – This is a reference from the Apostle Paul to Zech 8:16, so it is an ancient truth, not a new thing. This is said to remind us that lying has always been a problem since the fall of man. It is also, of course, the ninth commandment (Ex 20:16). Lying is a big deal, and those who are dealing with compulsive behaviors or addictions are usually excellent liars. They lie to others, they lie to themselves and they lie to God. In this admonition, God is pleading with us to quit lying because when one believer lies it damages all believers.

The Exercise – In the first part of this exercise discuss your lying habits. Detail out what you lie to others about, what you would lie to yourself about and what you would lie to God about. Be honest about how successful you were at lying, make an assessment on how good you became at speaking and living in lies. Back then, did you believe you were fooling anybody? Talk about the damage your lies did to your relationships, your work situation and your spiritual relationships, including God. Was it worth it?

Next, write about what you still lie about today and what you no longer lie about. Itemize the lies you continue to tell within your closest two or three relationships, include any lies you have told your sponsor or mentor. Do you believe you are "getting away with it" within those relationships?

Finally write about your desire to give up lying. Are you willing to suffer the consequences of truth telling? What might some of those consequences be? Are you afraid of losing someone or something of great significance, and who or what might they be? How much have you worked with God through prayer and meditation to deal with your lying problem? How often do you discuss this with your sponsor, mentor or other close believing friends or loved ones? Are you concerned about the damage you might be doing, or the legacy you might be leaving for any children you have?

To get the benefit of doing this exercise, we must be brutally honest and very thorough, or we will short-change ourselves!

Sponsor Notes: _____

_____

_____

Useful Feeling Words:

- Ashamed, Guilty, Humiliated, Exposed, Vulnerable

Useful Attitudinal Words:

- Rebellious, Disobedient, Anxious, Evasive, Obstinate

My Pre-exercise Notes: _____

_____

_____

_____

_____

The suggested step for Exercise 16 is Step 9.

Exercise 17

2 Corinthians 10:5

Capturing our Thoughts

2 Cor 10:5 - We destroy arguments and every lofty opinion raised against the knowledge of God, and take every thought captive to obey Christ. ESV

Guiding Commentary – In the context of recovery, this scripture acts as an instruction of major significance. In our thought life we are prone to lies, fantasies and prideful thoughts crossing our minds. These types of thoughts are raised up in our minds and directly contradict God and His word. In this scripture we are told to test these thoughts against the word of God, and whenever we know and understand that we are in error in our thinking we are to volitionally choose Christ's way in obedience. Too often we have found ourselves acting on our sinful thoughts leading maybe to momentary pleasures, but usually to destructive behaviors. This scripture instructs us to capture such thoughts to avoid destruction, much like trapping a wolf that is destroying a farmer's innocent sheep. We are to take these thoughts and confess them to Christ; we are not to act on them.

The Exercise – Discuss your thought life before you decided to deal with your problems or issues. Talk about what kinds of fantasies you indulged in; were they sexual, about money or control of others, or maybe about running away from life or even suicide. Perhaps you even considered the possibility of death of a loved one like a spouse or parent. Where did these thoughts lead to? Did you ever consider comparing your thoughts against God's word, and what did you do about that?

How are you doing now with your thought life? Do you still fantasize or speculate on the future. What do you do with all the ungodly thoughts that cross your mind? Are you still trying to dismiss them under your own willpower? How successful have you been? Do they continue to come back and haunt you?

Speak to what you might do with the ungodly parts of your current thought life now you have seen this instruction in new ways.

Sponsor Notes: _____

_____

_____

Useful Feeling Words:

- Confused, Guilty, Exposed, Encouraged, Enlightened

Useful Attitudinal Words:

- Avoiding, Hiding, Escapism, No, Embarrassment

My Pre-exercise Notes: _____

_____

_____

_____

_____

The suggested step for Exercise 17 is Step 10.

Exercise 18

1 Corinthians 10:13

Dealing with Temptations

1 Cor 10:13 - No temptation has overtaken you that is not common to man. God is faithful, and he will not let you be tempted beyond your ability, but with the temptation he will also provide the way of escape, that you may be able to endure it. ESV

Guiding Commentary – From this scripture we can see that we will all be tempted, and temptation is one of our enemy's primary tools of warfare. It is the tool he used to try to bring Christ down before His ministry even got started. Because of this it is believed by some scholars that temptation is Satan's most potent tool. As we can see in this passage, God has limited the enemies of our soul, in that they can only tempt us up to a level and in ways which God knows we can bear. With every temptation that God allows, He also provides a way out of it. So when we are tempted what are we to do? We could succumb, as we have done so many times, or we can look for the escape mechanism that God has provided for us. It is as if God has personally designed temptation and escape plans for us, but this is not true. Let us be sure to never blame God for our temptations, but to thank Him that he limits them and opens a door for a godly response from us.

It is also wise to note that, while God will not tempt us Himself, He will put us in a place where we can be tempted, as He did to Jesus. (Mk 1:12) He may use Satan, or the world system or even our own self-centered nature to as a tool in His hands to fulfill His purpose for our lives.

The Exercise – Talk about all the major temptations you have experienced in your life. Try to categorize them into attacks of the enemy, the influence of the world system or internally originating in your own heart. Assess how well you did with these in the past, and how well you are doing with them now.

Assist your sponsor or mentor by describing how severe these attacks of temptation were in the past versus now. Were you even aware that you were being tempted? Have your major temptations changed over time? What were you more tempted by earlier in your life compared to today? Are you experiencing new temptations? If so what are they and how severe are the attacks? When you are tempted now, do you look for the door of escape?

Finally add any other personal experiences about temptations that you believe might be useful to your advisor.

Sponsor Notes: _____

_____

_____

Useful Feeling Words:

- Confused, Guilty, Exposed, Encouraged, Enlightened

Useful Attitudinal Words:

- Apathetic, Evasive, Detached, Disinterested, Resigned

My Pre-exercise Notes: _____

_____

_____

_____

The suggested step for Exercise 18 is Step 10.

Exercise 19

Ezekiel 36:25-27

Getting a Heart of Flesh

Ezek 36:25-27 - I will sprinkle clean water on you, and you shall be clean from all your uncleannesses, and from all your idols I will cleanse you. And I will give you a new heart, and a new spirit I will put within you. And I will remove the heart of stone from your flesh and give you a heart of flesh. And I will put my Spirit within you, and cause you to walk in my statutes and be careful to obey my rules. ESV

Guiding Commentary – This is the great prophecy about the coming of what is called the "Age of Grace", the church age that we live in when God sends His Holy Spirit to live in us and we have a heart of flesh, instead of hard hearts of stone. It can also be applied to those of us in recovery. When we are far from God, and acting in our compulsions, we often have a developed an affinity for other gods (idols); examples are drugs, pornography, work, material possessions or our spouses. God says that when we do these things we develop a "heart of stone", often also called a hard heart. This heart of stone is characterized by things like uncaring attitudes, self-centeredness and willful denial of the truth. God promises that if we turn to Him he will cleanse us with water, living water, which is Jesus (Jn 4:13-14), who will cleanse us from the inside. He will give us a new heart, taking our "heart of stone" and replacing it with a "heart of flesh". His Spirit, which comes to reside inside us, will lead us into more righteous living, described in our text as walking in His statutes or rules.

The Exercise – Go back to the time in your life, (which might even be now), when you had a "heart of stone". Talk about your uncaring attitudes, self-centered behaviors and denials; try to identify any idols that you worshipped instead of the one true God. As you identify these character defects, list them in a way where you can then link the spiritual or relational result with them. (For example, you might have been uncaring toward a spouse, and when they were sick you still spent more time "acting out" than "being there" for them, resulting in a lack of intimacy.) Be detailed and as thorough in your work here as possible as it reveals things that are useful as you continue to work through your recovery.

The next part of this exercise is to see where God has already changed your stony heart and made it softer. Describe how your old attitudes, beliefs and values have been replaced by more godly attributes. Help your sponsor or mentor, and yourself, to understand how far you have come in your recovery. Speak to any sense of being a cleaner person, from a spiritual perspective. Finally write out a detailed prayer of thanks to God for what He has done so far for you. Praise him for giving you a "heart of flesh", and be specific about what you think He has helped you with so far.

Sponsor Notes: _____

_____

_____

Useful Feeling Words:

- Ashamed, Pain, Frustrated, Fearful, Guilty

Useful Attitudinal Words:

- Gratitude, Hard-hearted, Rebelliousness, Obstinate, Prideful

My Pre-exercise Notes: _____

_____

_____

_____

_____

The suggested step for Exercise 19 is Step 2.

Exercise 20

1 Corinthians 15:33

Keeping Good Company

1 Cor 15:33 - Do not be deceived: "Bad company ruins good morals." ESV

Guiding Commentary – Most of us in adulthood would agree with the last part of this simple verse. However, some of us make choices of friends and acquaintances as if we either don't believe that "bad company corrupts good morals" or believe that we can't be deceived about other people's character or morals. The truth is clear; we can be deceived by others about their moral makeup. It is also true that even if we can see somebody's bad side we so often believe that we can protect ourselves from their corrupting nature. This scripture says it well in a very black and white way. To paraphrase it: **When you hang out with immoral people you will be corrupted.**

The Exercise – Spend some time going back into your past, including your childhood, and think about all the people you used to hang out with. Pick out the people who influenced you to engage in immoral activities. Immoral activities include all the normal things of course, but don't forget some of the so-called "harmless" things we all did as kids. Examples might be hurtful practical jokes, name calling, cheating on tests, disobeying parents, looking at pornography with the neighbor kids, raiding someone's liquor cabinet, and so on. Now start to list these individuals from the past, along with approximately how old you were, what kinds of things you got into with them or because of them. (If you can't remember their name, just call them by an alias for this exercise.) If you can recall the feelings you had doing some of these things, then include them. (For example, looking at porn for a boy might be pleasurable, or putting down an ugly girl might feel like fun for another girl) Review your work and make some notes for discussion on any patterns of choices in friends or behaviors that you notice.

In the last part of this exercise, think about any immorality, or compulsive behaviors, you have been involved in recently and determine if you have been influenced into getting involved in them, or staying in them, by somebody. List the person and activity with any other comments you may have. Does this list concern you? If it does, what are you going to do about it?

Finally, are you being proactive about seeking friendships with individuals who show reasonably good moral character? Can you list some individuals that you may have met, but not befriended, that would be good people to be around? Will you pursue a relationship with these people?

Sponsor Notes: _____

_____

_____

Useful Feeling Words:

- Ashamed, Annoyed, Duped, Unworthy, Encouraged

Useful Attitudinal Words:

- Agreeable, Corrupt, Rebelliousness, Obstinate, Prideful

My Pre-exercise Notes: _____

_____

_____

_____

_____

The suggested step for Exercise 20 is Step 6.

Exercise 21

James 1:19-21

Moral Filth and Anger

James 1:19-21 - Know this, my beloved brothers: let every person be quick to hear, slow to speak, slow to anger; for the anger of man does not produce the righteousness that God requires. Therefore put away all filthiness and rampant wickedness and receive with meekness the implanted word, which is able to save your souls. ESV.

Guiding Commentary – God delivers an interesting perspective on anger through His servant James here. The book of James is hugely practical and full of biting truth, this is no exception. Here we are given an instruction about being a listener first, being slow to respond and being slow to allow anger to direct our actions. God says through this passage that our human anger does not produce right leaning actions, called righteousness in these verses. Then He says that because of this last truth, we ought to get rid of moral filth and replace it with the word of God, because this action will "save" us! The Greek word translated as "save" here is "**sozo**", which means "heal" so we can understand that when God uses the word "save" in this passage the context is that we will be healed from the effect our human anger has on us.

For us in recovery we can see the linkage between three things we experience as we work our recovery programs. All of us in recovery are attempting to get rid of impurities of some kind (called here filthiness and rampant wickedness) from inside of us, because we know these impurities are the source of our acting out behaviors. We also know that we must replace these impurities with pure things, and there is nothing purer, that we can use, than the word of God. And finally, it is very common for those in recovery to have unacceptable levels of anger in our lives, and we experience life through our angry responses, as do those who have had to put up with us. God here is explaining that the source of much of our anger is the moral filth we hang on to in our souls. Some individuals in recovery, even when faced with statements from those around them, deny that they experience life though anger. If you are one of these, you are urged to take a deep hard look at this with some trusted godly advisers.

44

The Exercise – Ponder on the subject of impurities inside you for a while and see if you can link them to anger in your life. Then write about what the Holy Spirit has helped you understand about yourself.

To help, here are some examples. Have you become angry when someone won't give in to your desires? Have you become angry because life isn't treating you fairly? Have you become angry with God because you thought you deserved something and He didn't give it to you? Think about things in the context of lust of the eyes, lust of the flesh and pride; which are three major impurities in our soul.

Sponsor Notes: _____

_____

_____

Useful Feeling Words:

- Anger, Hateful, Ashamed, Tempted, Deceived

Useful Attitudinal Words:

- Bitterness, Resentment, Prideful, Disobedient, Burdened

My Pre-exercise Notes: _____

_____

_____

_____

_____

The suggested step for Exercise 21 is Step 4.

Exercise 22

Galatians 6:1-2

Being Thankful For Others

Gal 6:1-2 - Brothers, if anyone is caught in any transgression, you who are spiritual should restore him in a spirit of gentleness. Keep watch on yourself, lest you too be tempted. Bear one another's burdens, and so fulfill the law of Christ. ESV

Guiding Commentary – All of us have been "caught in a transgression" and most of us understand how important it is to have grace-filled people around us at that time. This scripture admonishes all Christians to work on restoring those who have fallen into the traps of sins. In our context in recovery, we are to work on helping those trapped in their compulsions and addictions to overcome them, whilst also being careful that we don't get sucked into something we ought not do. When we share in the burdens of our fellow travelers in the recovery journey, when we assist them in moving forward, we are fulfilling the law of Christ, which in this context is to love God (in obedience) and our neighbor.

The Exercise – In this exercise we want to look at our past and acknowledge who has helped us, then look at today and see who we are helping.

Go back to the time that you first entered recovery. Perhaps you were caught in "acting out", or maybe you found yourself in jail, or lying in the gutter, or possibly even decided you simply had to deal with a problem. Who did you reach out to? Who was there to help you? Spend some time describing the circumstances that pushed you into recovery, and identify the people that are in your story. There may be people who caught you "acting out", or others that prayed for you, or others that just listened and still others that took you to meetings or a counselor. List them by name, and what they did for you, including even the smallest service they provided. Move forward into your first few months of recovery, and list the people that God brought into your life and how they contributed to your healing.

Now move on and start listing the people that you are helping in the same way, name them and write down what you are doing for them.

Finally write out a personal prayer of thanks for others. In this prayer acknowledge all the people on your lists by name, and acknowledge that it is God who coordinates these things, the meetings, the relationships and the healing, in your life. In this prayer, if you want to be an instrument of God's healing in the lives of others, ask Him to send you people who would benefit from your experiences and people who need to hear your story.

Sponsor Notes: _____

_____

_____

Useful Feeling Words:

- Happy, Elated, Thankful, Blessed, Joyous

Useful Attitudinal Words:

- Gratefulness, Helpfulness, Hopeful, Encouragement, Joyful

My Pre-exercise Notes: _____

_____

_____

_____

_____

The suggested step for Exercise 22 is Step 12.

Exercise 23

John 5:5-6

<u>Wanting to be Healed</u>

John 5:5-6 - One man was there who had been an invalid for thirty-eight years. When Jesus saw him lying there and knew that he had already been there a long time, he said to him, "Do you want to be healed?" ESV

<u>Guiding Commentary</u> – In this scripture we see the case of a man who has been ill for a long time who is asked that old recovery question, "Do you want to get well?" His response is one that is typical of a person who is in recovery and throws up barriers to their healing. He doesn't say "yes" to this simple question, he says "yes, but" by blaming others for not helping him, and others again for getting in his way. Just like some of us, he provides excuses for not doing what he needs to do as his part of his healing. The good news is that Jesus heals him anyway, and does it to glorify God.

<u>The Exercise</u> – The question asked by Jesus is one that every person who enters into a recovery program or personal counseling faces, "Do you want to get well?"

Think back to the time when you began counseling or recovery. Did somebody ask you that question in some form? Record, as best you can, the circumstances surrounding this question. Highlight dates, people, events, where you were emotionally speaking, include relational issues you were having and as many other facets of your life at that time as you can remember. Be assured that this question was asked of you, and most likely more than once, even though you may not remember it easily. Try to estimate how many years you had been ill.

Did you answer "yes" to this question back then, or did you prevaricate? Did you say "yes, but", and throw up all kinds of reasons for not accepting healing? The man by the pool had literally thousands of chances to get in the pool, but didn't. Was that you, or is that you now? Have you had many chances to move forward into healing; and not done so? Describe times when you have faced that question "Do you want to get well" and not been able to answer "yes". Address the issue we see in the story, which is that the sick man was comfortable in his sick condition and so he didn't put forth the effort needed to get into the pool. Have you been comfortable in your condition, in your illness, in your compulsions or addictions, so comfortable that you would rather stay sick than take the action you need to for healing?

If you have answered "yes", write down the story (or stories) of when you first chose to step out of your comfort zone and do the work, or as 12-steppers say "work the program".

Sponsor Notes: _____

_____

_____

Useful Feeling Words:

- Powerless, Hopeless, Unworthy, Forgotten, Damaged

Useful Attitudinal Words:

- Laziness, Blaming, Hopelessness, Victimhood, Irresponsibility

My Pre-exercise Notes: _____

_____

_____

_____

The suggested step for Exercise 23 is Step 3.

Exercise 24

Judges 2:11-12

<u>Don't Turn Back</u>

Judg 2:11-12 - And the people of Israel did what was evil in the sight of the Lord and served the Baals. And they abandoned the Lord, the God of their fathers, who had brought them out of the land of Egypt. They went after other gods, from among the gods of the peoples who were around them, and bowed down to them. And they provoked the Lord to anger. ESV

<u>Guiding Commentary</u> – The book of Judges is a great study for those in recovery. It is the story of people who have been delivered out of bondage (called Egypt in our scripture) who then in their new freedom turn away from God and go back into bondage. It is a story of relapse; it is a story of turning away from the healer; it is a story of being freed from one form of slavery and replacing it with another and finally it is a story of the spiritual consequences of turning away from God. Isn't that so like us in recovery, we get relief and healing from our struggles or our bondage, then we forget God? Things get easier for us, and so we relapse, some of us succumb to temptation, and some of us choose new bondages. Then we wonder why life takes a bad turn. It is because we don't remember that God loves us so much that even when we "provoke Him to anger" through turning away, He will discipline us, for our benefit.

<u>The Exercise</u> – Think back through your time in recovery. It is likely that you have experienced some of the things described above. Write out your personal story of getting relief or healing from your struggles, and then relapsing or falling back into your compulsions again or replacing one problem with another. Detail out as many of these as you can and as you do, look for God's hand in the form of discipline that you may have received from Him. This discipline could be in the form of lost marriages or other relationships, lost jobs, financial problems, illnesses or even jail time.

Be thorough in your work, it is very emotionally and spiritually healthy for us to connect what we have chosen to do in our lives, and see how God responds. As you finish this exercise, reflect on God's love for you in this context of our failures and His discipline. Then write a <u>personal</u> statement describing the way He has shown this love. Begin this statement with this wording:

My name is {your name}, I know God loves me because……

Sponsor Notes: _____

_____

_____

Useful Feeling Words:

- Repentant, Damaged, Unworthy, Shame, Guilt

Useful Attitudinal Words:

- Irresponsibility, Helplessness, Powerlessness, Undisciplined, Resentment

My Pre-exercise Notes: _____

_____

_____

_____

The suggested step for Exercise 24 is Step 7.

Exercise 25

2 Corinthians 7:10

Godly or Worldly Sorrow

2 Cor 7:10 - For godly grief produces a repentance that leads to salvation without regret, whereas worldly grief produces death. ESV

Guiding Commentary – So many of us enter recovery more than once, and it is this issue of "sorrow" that is at the center of the reason why recovery doesn't "stick" at first. Our scripture tells us that real sorrow (grief), which is godly sorrow, produces repentance without regret, whereas worldly sorrow produces death. When we have sorrow about what we have done there is a fork in the road ahead of us. The godly fork leads to internal change, healing and a healthy fear of returning to where we have just been. The worldly fork leads us nowhere but back to our lives of rebellion and disobedience, and probably back to our compulsions or addictions. We most likely will try to change some of our behaviors, but because we are not really sorry about violating God's ordinances, nothing really changes; we most often drive our compulsions underground for a while. In the world of addiction language, we never really reached our "bottoms"; we are just sorry we got caught!

A sign of godly sorrow is "repentance without regret". This is when we are truly sorry and are dealing with our troubles, and have no sense of regret about confessing or being caught or accepting our consequences. In fact, repentance without regret usually leads to thankfulness.

The Exercise – If you are relatively new to recovery this is an exercise where you search your heart, look inside to see what is there. Think about all the things you are doing, or have been doing and honestly answer if you are filled with godly sorrow or worldly sorrow or even no sorrow. Write out the circumstances of your issues being exposed, what were your feelings at that time? Were you just sorry you got caught? Or did you have a gut wrenching realization of the depths of your problems and how you were breaking God's commands? Describe as many of the emotions, thoughts, convictions and attitudes you experienced during the process of your heart being filled with sorrow.

For those who have been in recovery for some time this exercise is different. Yes, go back and do what a newbie does in the "sorrow review" described above, but add something. Add a description of how sorry you are today. Describe how you have repentance "without regret" and what that means to you. What would you recommend a "newbie" does as they come into recovery and are experiencing the first signs of sorrow?

Sponsor Notes: _____

_____

_____

Useful Feeling Words:

- Sorry, Regret, Repentant, Unworthy, Ashamed, Guilty

Useful Attitudinal Words:

- Helplessness, Powerlessness, Bitterness, Resentment, Challenged

My Pre-exercise Notes: _____

_____

_____

_____

_____

The suggested step for Exercise 25 is Step 1.

Exercise 26

Matthew 6:25(a) and 33

<u>Solving Anxiety</u>

Matt 6:25(a) - Therefore I tell you, do not be anxious about your life. 33 But seek first the kingdom of God and his righteousness, and all these things will be added to you. ESV

<u>Guiding Commentary</u> – This is the beginning and ending of a section of the "Sermon on the Mount" that deals with anxiety. Jesus, in His role as sovereign healer gives us His prescription on how to deal with worry/burdens/cares/anxieties. From a recovery perspective, He says to seek God and the solution will come to you.

In modern psychology there is a developing school of thought that suggests that all our troubles are sourced in our anxieties. In short, it is thought that we become fearful or anxious about something and so we seek a remedy to fix it. For example we may be anxious that a certain person won't approve of us, so we self medicate with alcohol. Another common example might be that a man becomes anxious that he won't relate to women, so he seeks the constant approval found in pornography. A woman might be anxious that other women will think badly of her unless she has a pristine home, so she becomes a cleaning junkie.

In Christian recovery we address this in our own way. We agree with Jesus that the solution to all our troubles or anxieties are found in God's guidance. Therefore we recommend seeking His kingdom, which is the rule and reign of Christ in our souls, and his righteousness, which is doing things His way. Because this scripture says that this is the way anxiety in our life is solved.

<u>The Exercise</u> – In this exercise we will focus on the question "Do you believe God?" It is a fundamental truth about our recovery through Christ, His work in our life and our obedience to His instructions, that if we don't believe Him, our unbelief becomes a barrier to the healing we desperately desire.

Write a comprehensive statement about the depth of your belief that in your life God will do what He says in our focus scripture. Be honest about where you are on the belief spectrum of no belief/no confidence to unconditional belief/total confidence. Write a prayer for your unbelief, include in this prayer an expression of thankfulness for the fact that God respects an honest statement of belief more than a sham lie. Pray this for yourself each day for one week.

Now take this to a meeting between you and your personal mentor/sponsor or counselor to discuss the role of belief in your recovery.

Sponsor Notes: _____

_____

_____

Useful Feeling Words:

- Depressed, Anxious, Disillusioned, Isolated, Lost

Useful Attitudinal Words:

- Apostate, Unbelief, Contempt, Disbelief, Ignorant

My Pre-exercise Notes: _____

_____

_____

_____

The suggested step for Exercise 26 is Step 3.

Exercise 27

John 3:19-21

<u>Light or Darkness</u>

John 3:19-21 - And this is the judgment: the light has come into the world, and people loved the darkness rather than the light because their deeds were evil. For everyone who does wicked things hates the light and does not come to the light, lest his deeds should be exposed. But whoever does what is true comes to the light, so that it may be clearly seen that his deeds have been carried out in God. ESV

<u>Guiding Commentary</u> – This is a part of what is probably the most important conversation ever recorded (Jn 3:1-21 – Jesus with Nicodemus). In it Jesus defines the judgment for us, this is not the judgment as in one person determining the fate of another, this is the internal judgment that we all face. The Greek word translated here as "judgment" sheds some light on this for us and is helpful to those of us in recovery; it is "krisis". Each person that ever existed faces a personal crisis, called here a judgment, and sometimes called a condemnation, it is the classic crisis of faith; **do I choose light or darkness**? In this scripture, the writer John, under the guidance of the Holy Spirit, even identifies this as a crisis where we are caught choosing between "The Light", meaning Jesus, and darkness. Our scripture tells us that every time we choose an act of darkness, (doing evil), we are rejecting Jesus. That is contrasted with practicing the truth, which is acting in godly ways, which then proves how God is acting in and through us.

<u>The Exercise</u> – Think back to the days you were acting out. Were you aware that each time you chose a deed of darkness you were committing an act of evil, and that you were rejecting Jesus? Some of us would admit that we knew this, some of us may never have thought of it, and some of us may still be in denial that our actions were evil. For this exercise detail out some of your acts of darkness, being as open and honest as you can; admit or deny that you knew fully what you were doing and that it was evil. Try to identify who you were hurting.

Write out a prayer of confession to God about these things. Even though He knows it all, be detailed and specific about the facts. Be sure to include a section of your prayer that covers your personal repentance for your deeds of darkness,

56

and most importantly for your rejection of Jesus. After you have written out your prayer, read it alone to God, and then spend at least 30 minutes in solitude with Him. Read it at least once each day, and meditate for at least 5 minutes, until you next meet with your personal Christian guide.

Record or journal your thoughts and feelings each time after your period of meditation for discussion later with your sponsor, counselor or mentor.

Sponsor Notes: _____

_____

_____

Useful Feeling Words:

* Depressed, Anxious, Disillusioned, Isolated, Lost

Useful Attitudinal Words:

* Denial, Disbelief, Ignorant, Avoidance, Willful

My Pre-exercise Notes: _____

_____

_____

_____

_____

The suggested step for Exercise 27 is Step 4.

Exercise 28

Jonah 2:8-9

Make a New Vow

Jonah 2:8-9 - Those who pay regard to vain idols forsake their hope of steadfast love. But I with the voice of thanksgiving will sacrifice to you; what I have vowed I will pay. Salvation belongs to the Lord! ESV

Guiding Commentary – The prophet Jonah was a troubled and rebellious man, and as such was on the tough end of some discipline from God. One of the disciplines he had to go through was being swallowed by a great fish, and he prayed a psalm of thanksgiving from inside the fish. Our two verses are the last part of that psalm.

One of the spiritually healthy ways to think about our compulsive behaviors is that they are idols; things we prefer over God. Here we see Jonah reminding us that clinging to our idols draws us away from God, and consequently from His love. God's love can be described as the source of His healing power, the very thing we need from Him in our recovery. (God is love – 1 Jn 4:8) In the second part of the scripture we're using we see Jonah declaring that he will sacrifice, meaning place his love for God over his love for his idol (himself), and will keep his word, the promise he made to God.

For us in Christian recovery this is a step we take when we choose to turn over our will to God in the matter of dealing with our problems. We will sacrifice our own chasing after idols for doing life God's way, and putting Him and His word first.

The Exercise – For this exercise begin by writing out a key word(s) with a simple dictionary style description of each of your compulsive behaviors. Normally those in recovery have one primary and at least two secondary compulsions that are dealing with. For example you may be a people-pleaser that drinks and is a perfectionistic home cleaner. Another example is that you might be a sex-addict that does drugs sometimes, and drinks extensively.

Using this list write out a detailed prayer in the style of Jonah 2:8-9 above. Begin your prayer with a confession that you have been chasing worthless idols, naming the ones you have described in the first part of this exercise. Then, write out your personal promise to God (as part of your prayer) that you are going to give Him your best efforts in leaving them behind, as you turn to Him for help. In this promise, spell out what attitude(s) you will be bringing to the table to help you sustain yourself in the work you know will need to be done. End the prayer with a declaration of who God is to you.

Pray and meditate on this for at least five days, and then discuss it with a godly advisor.

Sponsor Notes: _____

_____

_____

Useful Feeling Words:

- Afraid, Ashamed, Guilty, Painful, Victimized

Useful Attitudinal Words:

- Isolate, Denial, Repentant, Rebellious, Disobedient

My Pre-exercise Notes: _____

_____

_____

_____

_____

The suggested step for Exercise 28 is Step 3.

Exercise 29

Ephesians 4:22-24

Putting on a New Self

Eph 4:22-24 - Put off your old self, which belongs to your former manner of life and is corrupt through deceitful desires, and be renewed in the spirit of your minds, and put on the new self, created after the likeness of God in true righteousness and holiness. ESV

Guiding Commentary – (Also see Col 3:9-11) The author of this scripture, the Apostle Paul, is giving us a great recovery message here. He begins this small section of scripture by telling us to look back at how we used to live, and lay aside that old person. That old person (old self) was, and still is, corrupted by deceiving lusts. We allow ourselves to create these deceiving lusts in us by believing lies; our own lies or the lies of others in the world, or even the lies of our unseen spiritual enemies. We are to be renewed by the putting on of a new self, a new self which is our old self being renewed in the spirit of our mind. This is when we replace the lies with the truth, with the result that we won't act according to the deceiving lusts any more, we will act more like Christ in righteous ways and godly actions. This is often called becoming Christlike, and it can only happen when we are guided by the Holy Spirit and in His power.

The Exercise – In this exercise we want to look at the lies that we believe existed in our lives in the past, and try to link any deceitful lusts we had to deal with because of them. Write out a description of these lies, and if they were internally generated or we absorbed them from the world (people we knew or other worldly sources) or even if we think we were given these lies by unseen spiritual forces. Then identify the deceitful lusts that sprang from these lies, particularly those that we acted on. (For example, if we believed it was okay to take extra prescription pills because of the lie they wouldn't harm us, then we started taking them and got hooked.)

Once we have completed this task then we can turn to how we have dealt with these deceptions. Write out how you have progressed from a corrupt old self to a new self. Do this in the context of identifying old false beliefs, more commonly called lies, and replaced them with God's beliefs, more commonly called truth.

Talk about how you used do one thing (acting out) and now do something new and more godly.

Finally, write out a comparative statement of how you are more "Christlike" now than when you were in your personal pit. In your statement give God the credit where He should have it, and give yourself credit where you should. End it with a sentence describing how you feel about yourself today compared to back "then".

Sponsor Notes: _____

_____

_____

Useful Feeling Words:

- Embarrassed, Guilty, Betrayed, Uncomfortable, Uplifted

Useful Attitudinal Words:

- Strong, Weak, Disbelieving, Rebelliousness, Thankful

My Pre-exercise Notes: _____

_____

_____

_____

_____

The suggested step for Exercise 29 is Step 6.

Exercise 30

2 Kings 5:1-15

Responding to Powerlessness

2 Kings 5:1 - Naaman, commander of the army of the king of Syria, was a great man with his master and in high favor, because by him the Lord had given victory to Syria. He was a mighty man of valor, but he was a leper. **ESV**

Guiding Commentary – Read the whole story of Naaman in 1 Kings 5:1-15 before moving forward in this exercise. In this story we see a character, Naaman, a great and accomplished man of his time. Naaman has had extraordinary success in his life and has conquered everything before him (notice the scripture says this was through God!), but he has leprosy. Leprosy back then was a disease that always resulted in early death, there was no cure, and it was something that Naaman could not conquer. He was powerless! When we read the rest of the story, we see that Naaman had to be humbled by his circumstances to finally be cured by God. Notice that Naaman had to obey God, through instructions given to him by God's prophet Elisha, before he could be healed. It wasn't the river that cleaned him; it was God, in response to Naaman's obedience that cured him. The result was that Naaman was both physically cured and spiritually cured, and he gave glory to God because of it. Notice also that God used several people in this story to accomplish His purposes.

The Exercise – If you are new to recovery you may still be struggling with powerlessness and the personal pride that is stopping you from admitting that you can't control your compulsions. You are in the same position as Naaman was before he chose to accept his powerlessness and then accept God's offer of healing. If this is you, look around you and see if God has brought new people into your life to point you in a new direction, as He did for Naaman. If you can see some, write down their names and what they are telling you about how to deal with your situation. Now write out a prayer for yourself for God to help you gain a heart of willing obedience to these people that God is putting in your life.

If you are more of a recovery veteran, go back to your powerless days and record the names of some of the people who influenced you enough for you to finally admit your powerlessness. Write out how they helped you. How much did your agreeing to do what these people said to do help you? Speak, as you write, about your level of obedience to their instructions or suggestions; were you simply compliant or was it more? Do you recognize that they were given to you by God? Now write out a prayer of thanks to God, naming all those who had even a small part in your recovery, and what they did.

Sponsor Notes: _____

_____

_____

Useful Feeling Words:

- Powerless, Incapable, Hopeless, Expectant, Thankful

Useful Attitudinal Words:

- Rebelliousness, Gratefulness, Victimhood, Questioning, Prideful

My Pre-exercise Notes: _____

_____

_____

_____

_____

The suggested step for Exercise 30 is Step 1.

Exercise 31

Romans 1:18-20

<u>God is Evident – No excuses</u>

Rom 1:18-20 - For the wrath of God is revealed from heaven against all ungodliness and unrighteousness of men, who by their unrighteousness suppress the truth. For what can be known about God is plain to them, because God has shown it to them. For his invisible attributes, namely, his eternal power and divine nature, have been clearly perceived, ever since the creation of the world, in the things that have been made. So they are without excuse. ESV

<u>Guiding Commentary</u> – This can be a tough message to swallow for people in recovery. God states in this passage that He has made Himself evident to all of mankind from the beginning. This means that no human that has ever existed or will exist has an excuse for their ungodly and unrighteous behavior. To avoid being accountable, we as fallen humans, suppress the truth; truth that He exists, that He made it all, that He is all powerful, that He is in control and that He will judge us all in righteous anger. Some of us in recovery like to emphasize issues like family of origin, or having been abused, being rejected or abandoned as a child and many more things as being the reason for our sinful behaviors. We over emphasize and blame those things for our troubles, and we place only a small weighting on our own choices in our actions. We claim we have been driven into compulsions or addictions instead of voluntarily choosing our own destructive patterns. The truth is that we must acknowledge those past events that shaped our values, beliefs and attitudes, and use this knowledge to explain how we were set on certain courses, but we cannot honestly blame them for our actions. God has made Himself evident, and we are without excuse for what we have done, and maybe are still doing. Our response to this truth is that we must appeal to His mercy and ask for forgiveness for ignoring the evidences He has given to us.

<u>The Exercise</u> – In this exercise we must go back to our acting out days and look at what our values, beliefs and attitudes were at that time. Be sure that you try hard to identify your actual values etc, from back then, they will be evidenced by your actions. For example if you acted out sexually, then you had a value of "adultery is acceptable". Compare these old values etc, with what you think you knew about the word of God back then. Individuals coming out of acting out and into recovery

can usually identify several of these situations where they exhibited one value etc, but knew another. This is a truth about ourselves that demonstrates that the scripture above is accurate when God says we knew and are without excuse.

We must be careful not to let this "get to us", because this is a truth about every person, no one is exempt. When we do this exercise we are merely bringing this truth about ourselves into the light, and this is healing for us. Knowing this truth brings us closer to God, as it removes another barrier of denial from between us and Him.

Sponsor Notes: _____

_____

_____

Useful Feeling Words:

- Frustrated, Hurt, Shame, Guilt, Avoidant

Useful Attitudinal Words:

- Rebelliousness, Prideful, Disbelief, Denial, Seeking

My Pre-exercise Notes: _____

_____

_____

_____

_____

The suggested step for Exercise 31 is Step 4.

Exercise 32

John 8:10-11

Go and Sin No More

John 8:10-11 Jesus stood up and said to her, "Woman, where are they? Has no one condemned you?" She said, "No one, Lord." And Jesus said, "Neither do I condemn you; go, and from now on sin no more." ESV

Guiding Commentary – This is the very end of the story of the woman caught in adultery (Jn 8:1-11) and it has excellent recovery application for us. Many of us in recovery were "caught" in our deep compulsions, addictions and acting out, and were confronted with the truth, just like this woman. Some of us simply realized that we were out of control in some way, and entered recovery by our own choice; we effectively confronted or caught ourselves. No matter which way we did get into recovery, we can be sure the Holy Spirit had a role in it, even if we can't see it, because He has been given the job of conviction of sin in the current age. The point of this scripture is to tell us that Jesus, through the Holy Spirit, is telling us that He is not going to condemn us for our acting out. He acknowledges that we are acting out, and He releases us from condemnation but not the natural consequences of our actions. He simply says to all of us, stop acting out.

The Exercise – Write the story of how you got into recovery. Were you "caught" or "confronted" by others? Did you sense at that time that they were trying to help you, or were they trying to punish you in some way, as they were trying to do to the woman in the story? Did you check yourself into recovery, if so, then what caused you to want to change or stop your bad habits? In either case, what part did the Holy Spirit play in this big change of direction in your life?

As you moved forward did you sense you were being judged and condemned by others or God? After some time did you sense anything different in the way people or God were treating you? Did you gain an understanding or sense that God was not condemning you, and that He was asking you to stop acting out? (Look up Rom 8:1) If you did not, what do you think is the reason for that? If this is still a struggle go to God in prayer and ask Him to search your heart so that you can identify the barrier to you accepting His free gift of gracious forgiveness. This struggle would be a great topic to discuss with your sponsor the next time you meet with him or her.

Sponsor Notes: _____

_____

_____

Useful Feeling Words:

- Shame, Guilt, Afraid, Troubled, Confused

Useful Attitudinal Words:

- Condemning, Judgmental, Punishing, Graceful, Shaming

My Pre-exercise Notes: _____

_____

_____

_____

_____

The suggested step for Exercise 32 is Step 7.

Exercise 33

Galatians 6:7-10

<u>Sowing and Reaping</u>

Gal 6:7-10 - Do not be deceived: God is not mocked, for whatever one sows, that will he also reap. For the one who sows to his own flesh will from the flesh reap corruption, but the one who sows to the Spirit will from the Spirit reap eternal life. And let us not grow weary of doing good, for in due season we will reap, if we do not give up. So then, as we have opportunity, let us do good to everyone, and especially to those who are of the household of faith. ESV

<u>Guiding Commentary</u> – The concept of "sowing and reaping" is well proven in our recovery stories. However, we usually focus on our acting out, and the bad treatment we have received from others, when we think about this. In this scripture we are asked to proactively and persistently go and sow good seeds, and in this way our lives will become better over time. We are encouraged to do good to all people, particularly other believers. The beginning of this effort in our lives in recovery is when we make amends to those we have hurt. Making amends involves the sowing of truth in our relationships with the godly motivation of getting right with others. It involves the giving and accepting of forgiveness in all those awkward situations from our past. God will always honor this in the individuals who practice it.

<u>The Exercise</u> – In this exercise we want to write out the names of the top ten people with whom we need to make amends, or have already made amends. If you have yet to make amends, write beside each name what you have to make amends for, and then write a short opening script for when you do meet them. If the person is not available because they have passed away or are geographically distant, or it is not advisable to meet with them as agreed with your sponsor, write out what you would say if they were.

If you have already made amends with all or some of your top ten, then write out what happened as you made amends and describe the results. Comment on how you think and feel it went, then comment on the long term effects of this activity on your relationships. Do you believe your everyday life got easier or less stressful as a result of making amends to others? Do you think that your life is richer and more joyful because you have been able to openly address the weaknesses and shortcomings in your past behaviors with those who were affected? Be sure to comment on how it is better.

Finally, write down what advice you would give to others struggling with making amends.

Sponsor Notes: _____

_____

_____

Useful Feeling Words:

- Afraid, Cautious, Willing, Pained, Troubled

Useful Attitudinal Words:

- Fearful, Punishment, Shaming, Expectant, Willing

My Pre-exercise Notes: _____

_____

_____

_____

_____

The suggested step for Exercise is 33 Step 8.

Exercise 34

Micah 6:8

Will of God

Mic 6:8 - He has told you, O man, what is good; and what does the Lord require of you but to do justice, and to love kindness, and to walk humbly with your God? ESV

Guiding Commentary – Have you ever wondered what the will of God is? In this statement God tells us. It is not a complete description of the entire will of God for each individual, it is a global statement that all of mankind is covered by. There are three components:

- Act with justice – each human is recognized as having equal value.
- Love and practice mercy – compassion, grace and forgiveness.
- Be humble – living without pride under God's guidance.

In the context of recovery these can be applied this way:

- God recognizes that each of us has equal and great value and He will treat us all with fair discipline, and He asks us to afford the same value to ourselves, toward those we are working with and those we have harmed.
- We are to be grace-filled toward ourselves and others, applying and receiving forgiveness and compassion wherever appropriate.
- We are to submit our wills to Almighty God, the one who created and designed us, and allow Him to do what only He can do in us.

The Exercise – In recovery we have to often come to terms with a new understanding that we are what scripture calls brokenhearted, and in need of the kind of justice God speaks of in his word.

For this written exercise answer the question, "Do you consider yourself in need of godly justice?" Start with a statement (for example, I do or I don't need godly justice) and then explain why or why not in one paragraph. In scripture, God instructs His followers to exhibit justice to the poor, blind, lame, fatherless, widows, orphans and more. Write out a statement describing your condition using some of those words. (For example, I am blind because I couldn't see how my behavior was hurting my wife.) Next write out a statement describing your need for mercy, compassion and forgiveness.

Finally write out a short prayer confessing your need for God to deliver you His merciful justice and asking Him to help you be, and stay, humble throughout whatever process He may put you through. Pray this prayer for yourself for a week, and if you are comfortable ask two or three other people to pray it with you over the same time period.

Sponsor Notes: _____

_____

_____

Useful Feeling Words:

- Compassionate, Joyful, Nervous, Wanting, Ready

Useful Attitudinal Words:

- Merciful, Punishment, Afraid, Expectant, Forgiving

My Pre-exercise Notes: _____

_____

_____

_____

_____

The suggested step for Exercise 34 is Step 3.

Exercise 35

Zephaniah 3:17

<u>When God Rejoices</u>

Zeph 3:17 - The Lord your God is in your midst, a mighty one who will save; He will rejoice over you with gladness; He will quiet you by his love; He will exult over you with loud singing. ESV

<u>Guiding Commentary</u> – This verse is a wonderful expression of how God wants to think, feel and act about us. In Zephaniah Chapter 3 God is assailing those who are apostate, turned away from Him. He tells them He is going to bring unbelievers against them as discipline for their sins, particularly their unbelief. Then He says that they will turn back to Him. It is after this return to the Lord that He speaks our focus verse.

Some of us arrive at the beginning of our Christian recovery, and some of us have practiced recovery but slipped in the faith part of it, to the point that could be considered apostate to some degree. If that is where we are, emotionally or spiritually speaking we must expect God to discipline us. This verse tells us how God will respond to our moving back toward Him.

He will be with us, He will use His might to help us, He will delight in us, He will bring us godly peace which quiets our soul and He will sing for joy over us. That last expression of God's love for us is actually a phrase scripture uses to speak of God's protection. It may sound strange to us, but He protects us by singing over us.

<u>The Exercise</u> – Take a look at the period in your life before you entered recovery and do some introspective thinking about what your attitude to God really was. Write about it, admit it if you were apostate at some level, feel free to ask those who knew you then to help you remember. Evidences of apostasy include disobedience to God's instructions, lack of personal spiritual disciplines in our day to day life (prayer, bible study, and church attendance for example) and apathy toward God. If you have experienced a spiritual relapse since you entered recovery write about that too.

Finally write about how you feel about this part of your life (use feeling words!), what you are going to do to avoid it happening again and what this verse means to you now that you know it exists and what it means.

Sponsor Notes: _____

_____

_____

Useful Feeling Words:

- Afraid, Anxious, Thankful, Expectant, Guilty

Useful Attitudinal Words:

- Punishment, Fearful, Ready, Hopefulness, Desiring

My Pre-exercise Notes: _____

_____

_____

_____

_____

The suggested step for Exercise 35 is Step 11.

Exercise 36

1 Samuel 12:20-23

<u>Your Part – His Promise</u>

1 Sam 12:20-23 - And Samuel said to the people, "Do not be afraid; you have done all this evil. Yet do not turn aside from following the Lord, but serve the Lord with all your heart. And do not turn aside after empty things that cannot profit or deliver, for they are empty. For the Lord will not forsake his people, for his great name's sake, because it has pleased the Lord to make you a people for himself. Moreover, as for me, far be it from me that I should sin against the Lord by ceasing to pray for you, and I will instruct you in the good and the right way. ESV

<u>Guiding Commentary</u> – Even though this message was for the people of Israel about 1050 BC, it has direct relevance today for those of us Christians in recovery. The message is clear. Don't fear, even though you have done all these evil things in the past, stick with God. Don't turn from His path, His ways and His instructions, because if you do, you will start chasing things that will not bring anything to help you, futile things. God will not abandon you, not because you deserve it, but because of His great name, by which we are called (Christ followers) and because He has chosen to make us His people. This is a great message of hope. If we do our part, which is to follow Him, He will be there for us.

<u>The Exercise</u> – Spend some time in reflection on this message and ask God to take this into your heart as if it were a personal letter from God to you. Think about not being full of fear over the future, about being determined to follow God and His ways, and about the futility that will be in your life if you get off track. Finally think about that promise that He is making to you. He won't abandon you, because to do so would tarnish His great name, and He has called you one of His people. (Read 1 Pet 2:3-10 as an affirmation of this)

Now write a personal letter to Christ in thanksgiving and praise for this personal letter to you. In it admit that you have done things in the past that brought you personal shame and guilt. Make a promise to Him that you are going to honestly do your best to follow Him and His ways, so that you will no longer chase after futile things. Thank Him for His promise to never abandon you and that He has called you "one of His people". Share this letter with any accountability partners you may have.

Sponsor Notes: _____

_____

_____

Useful Feeling Words:

- Worthy, Valued, Guilty, Uncondemned, Unique

Useful Attitudinal Words:

- Fearful, Resentment, Anxious, Pessimistic, Somber

My Pre-exercise Notes: _____

_____

_____

_____

_____

The suggested step for Exercise 36 is Step 11.

Exercise 37

Deuteronomy 8:5-6

<u>The Lord Disciplines</u>

Deut 8:5-6 - Know then in your heart that, as a man disciplines his son, the Lord your God disciplines you. So you shall keep the commandments of the Lord your God by walking in his ways and by fearing him. ESV

<u>Guiding Commentary</u> – This verse is part of a monologue from God to the Israelites as they moved out of bondage (Egypt) into a growth phase (Wilderness) with the future expectation of a better life (Promised Land). The whole story of God's rescuing of His people is a story of recovery and right in the middle of it we find this gem. In these two verses God tells us that during our journey we are to expect Him to discipline us as part of our growth after we have entered recovery. He says we are to "know" this in our heart; another way of understanding this is that we are to <u>believe</u> that God will discipline us. God then goes on to tell us that our proper response to this discipline is to obey His instructions and reverentially fear Him. While we can easily understand obedience, it can be hard to understand why we need to choose to fear Him, in this context. In a life of recovery, some of us will tend to backside occasionally (as the Israelites did in the wilderness). We are to understand that when we do this we will be disciplined by the Lord, and we are to fear His discipline. Some of the ways that God might do this include loss of parental rights, loss of health, loss of a job, loss of relationships or even jail time. He disciplines us because He loves us, as we love our own children. Let's not despise His discipline, let us embrace it, because when we receive it we know God is with us.

<u>The Exercise</u> – In this exercise we are to investigate whether we can see the Lord's discipline in our lives during recovery. As we came out of our own bondages, we all moved into some form of wilderness experience. This is the time in our recovery when we had most likely stopped "acting out" and were working on trying to do the right things the right way, meaning God's way. Most of us stumbled to some degree, and eventually began to see that there was a path to our own promised land, which we sometimes call healing. During the coming out of bondage and moving through our own wilderness we would sometimes be subject to the Lord's discipline.

Go back through your story, starting at the point of crisis, when you were confronted with the reality of your situation and look to see if you can spot the Lord's discipline. God most often uses others to discipline us, sometimes He uses circumstances and sometimes He convicts us through His Holy Spirit by exposing our sin to us. Write out as many of these situations as you can in reasonable detail, including dates, times, people and events in your life.

Sponsor Notes: _____

_____

_____

Useful Feeling Words:

- Angry, Oppressed, Frustrated, Sad, Stressed

Useful Attitudinal Words:

- Gladness, Punishment, Judgment, Victimhood, Gratefulness

My Pre-exercise Notes: _____

_____

_____

_____

_____

The suggested step for Exercise 37 is Step 3.

Exercise 38

Matthew 6:19-21

<u>Eternal Treasures</u>

Matt 6:19-21 - Do not lay up for yourselves treasures on earth, where moth and rust destroy and where thieves break in and steal, but lay up for yourselves treasures in heaven, where neither moth nor rust destroys and where thieves do not break in and steal. For where your treasure is, there your heart will be also. ESV

<u>Guiding Commentary</u> – These words are from the greatest sermon ever preached, which we call the "Sermon on the Mount", preached by Jesus as He completed the early part of His ministry. In these three verses Jesus is instructing us in something, pleading with us to take Him seriously and pointing out a great truth about our priorities. So many people only apply this to our materialistic ways and compare them to God's instruction to idolize only Him. In recovery we can see a wider application. In our days of acting out our hearts chased after worldly treasures. Examples might be pornography or romance novels for sexual thrills, gambling for a rush, drinking or drugging to get high and people-pleasing to manipulate others into relational appreciation. All of these kinds of things have no eternal worth, and all of them open the door to our unseen enemies who will "break in and steal". What will they steal? They will steal our joy; they will steal our peace of mind, our ability to rest and our healthy relationships. Jesus is trying to get us to understand that when we treasure Him and His ways, we will store treasures where they cannot be got at by our enemies. Some of these will be treasures that are stored in our hearts right now, and kept under the eternal protection of the Holy Spirit who resides in us, and that we will be taking with us as we enter heaven one day.

<u>The Exercise</u> – Go back into your past and write down a list of worldly treasures that you used to have. (It is okay to include material things too.) Now look at what you treasure today and see if they are eternal in nature. As you compare the before and after lists write down your thoughts, feelings and any impulses you might be sensing. (Impulses could include wanting to pray, go hug your children or even being tempted to go back into something.) Explore these impulses, thoughts and feelings with your advisor, sponsor or accountability partners.

Lastly, spend some time meditating, communicating with God, over what treasures you might want to pursue having in your future. Then write out a prayer to the Lord about these.

Sponsor Notes: _____

_____

_____

Useful Feeling Words:

- Thankful, Valued, Cherished, Informed, Relieved

Useful Attitudinal Words:

- Gratefulness, Listening, Gladness, Joy, Aware

My Pre-exercise Notes: _____

_____

_____

_____

_____

The suggested step for Exercise 38 is Step 12.

Exercise 39

Exodus 22:9

Payment of Restitution

Ex 22:9 - For every breach of trust, whether it is for an ox, for a donkey, for a sheep, for a cloak, or for any kind of lost thing, of which one says, 'This is it,' the case of both parties shall come before God. The one whom God condemns shall pay double to his neighbor. ESV

Guiding Commentary – During the "giving of the law" to the Israelites in the wilderness, the principle of restitution was established. Restitution is normally defined as "An act of repaying or compensating for loss, damage or injury." In our scripture, God says we are to pay restitution for "every breach of trust". For those of us in recovery we recognize this as "making amends".

The making of amends for a person going through some form of a recovery process, such as the 12 steps, can be a tortuous series of events. However, it is ordained by God as a method of restoring what has been lost or damaged. It is a completely necessary part of our personal healing. The making of amends speaks to the person receiving the amends that we have recognized that we breached a trust and that we stole, damaged or otherwise injured someone or something of value in the other person's life, and we are willing to make restitution. Some of us need to make financial or other material amends for what we have stolen or caused others to have lost economically speaking; but all of us in recovery must be willing to make relational amends. Mostly relational amends takes the form of confession coupled with the asking for forgiveness for our destructive actions against the other person.

God instructs us to do this, and we must be willing to do it in obedience to Him, for our own sakes.

The Exercise – If you have yet to begin making amends, write down about what you expect the future face-to-face meetings to be like. List some of your more significant "amendees" and detail out how you expect them to react. In your heart, are you willing to make amends? Write out your response to that question, and the reasons for it.

If you have already begun making amends, then write out the names of some of these "amendees" with a description of how the meetings and giving of amends went, and of course, their responses to your action of making restitution. Also include how you felt about things as you were making the amends, and then how you felt after it was initially over, and then also how you felt much later. Do you believe that when you made amends, even if they were not accepted, you were relieved of a burden of some kind? Add other comments you may wish to include.

Sponsor Notes: _____

_____

_____

Useful Feeling Words:

- Fearful, Relieved, Thankful, Burdened, Misunderstood

Useful Attitudinal Words:

- Powerlessness, Victimhood, Fearfulness, Anxious, Agitated

My Pre-exercise Notes: _____

_____

_____

_____

_____

The suggested step for Exercise 39 is Step 8.

Exercise 40

2 Samuel 9:6-7

<u>From Defeat to Restoration</u>

2 Sam 9:6-7 - And Mephibosheth the son of Jonathan, son of Saul, came to David and fell on his face and paid homage. And David said, "Mephibosheth!" And he answered, "Behold, I am your servant." And David said to him, "Do not fear, for I will show you kindness for the sake of your father Jonathan, and I will restore to you all the land of Saul your father, and you shall eat at my table always." ESV

<u>Guiding Commentary</u> – In verse 1 of this chapter from 2 Samuel, King David, after he had taken command of Israel made a promise, a very special promise. It was usual for a conquering king in those ancient times to kill the entire family of a vanquished king. Here David promises the one remaining descendent of Saul that he will not only let him live, but allow him into the royal presence to be part of the royal court and to "eat at his table always", and most importantly, David is going to restore everything to him. This is a picture of how God will treat us in recovery. We have to admit we have been defeated in life and will die in our misery without God's mercy. Then we must allow the One who has conquered death, King Jesus, to determine our fate. He stands ready to restore us and have us "eat at His table always". (Luke 22:30) Are you ready to accept this promise from God? To receive it all we have to do is to turn ourselves over to Him and follow His path. In recovery we have to admit we are defeated, that we are powerless and cannot manage our lives. God promises that when we begin to turn our lives over to Him, He will begin the work of restoration. In His grace He allows us to choose a life of defeat or a life eating at His table.

<u>The Exercise</u> – Did you know that when you were acting out you were acting as if you were an enemy of God? In this exercise talk about the time you decided to turn yourself over to God, when you admitted defeat and surrendered to Him. Talk about your understanding of what this means to you. If you didn't know you were once an enemy of God, how do you feel about that now, and how do you feel toward God who could see this in you?

If you are still acting out, does your attitude toward life, recovery and even God tell you something about yourself? Do you understand that you are acting as if you are an enemy of God? How do you think God ought to treat you while you are still in rebellion to Him? Would you like to eat fully at His table?

FYI – Eating at His table in the context of recovery means being fully restored, renewed and reconciled with Him and receiving things like peace, rest, encouragement, support, comfort and healing from past wounds.

Sponsor Notes: _____

_____

_____

Useful Feeling Words:

- Grateful, Expectant, Surrendered, Anxiety, Fearful

Useful Attitudinal Words:

- Thankfulness, Anxious, Fearfulness, Rebelliousness, Punishment

My Pre-exercise Notes: _____

_____

_____

_____

_____

The suggested step for Exercise 40 is Step 3.

Exercise 41

Acts 19:18

Full Disclosure

Acts 19:18 - Also many of those who were now believers came, confessing and divulging their practices. ESV

Guiding Commentary – This verse is part of a story with many spiritual facets, but the important part for us in recovery is the idea of full disclosure. When we read the full story (Acts 19:11-20) we can see that the people doing the confessing were responding to fear of God. When we in recovery face the prospect of having to disclose our stuff, we often have fear, and we particularly have fear when we are to disclose to those we have hurt. Some of us buckle under the strain of this fear and allow our shame and guilt to stop us from full disclosure. Most of us don't even consider fearing the Lord because we are so bound up in our emotions. In our acting out, the one person who feels the hurt the most is God, and we rarely consider that truth in our recovery work. In this verse we see all those who have done terrible things that would cause God to feel hurt come to Him and confess it all, they give a full disclosure. In verse 20 we see the result of this; the word of the Lord grows mightily. The relationship between the offenders and God is cleaned up and restored because of full disclosure. This is why when we make amends to others; we must do it with full disclosure. This will open the door to the possibility of a restored relationship, not guarantee it, just make it possible.

The Exercise – Some of us in recovery make the mistake of not confessing every relevant item in one meeting when we disclose our transgressions to those we have harmed. We prefer to only bring up a few items, and save the rest until later, hoping to spread and reduce the pain of the event. When we do this it is like having our wisdom teeth out one at a time. The best method of full disclosure is to get as much out as possible when the time is right, in this way the pain is dealt with quickly and we hope, finally.

Write about your disclosure experiences. Name some of those to whom you have made amends and disclosed things to and how it went. Talk about the things you did that resulted in hurt in their life, and how you dealt with disclosing your part in those things. Discuss how the relationship was before you started acting out, what it became as a result of acting out and what it became after your disclosure. Make some comments on if "fear of the Lord" was a consideration in your disclosures.

If you haven't gone through a disclosure, talk about who you have to disclose to, what has to be disclosed, what you are feeling about having to do this and if you have considered fear of God as a factor. Does bringing God into your disclosure change your sense of fear or concerns? If so, what changes?

Sponsor Notes: _____

_____

_____

Useful Feeling Words:

- Anxiety, Fearful, Concerned, Ashamed, Exposed

Useful Attitudinal Words:

- Anxious, Fearfulness, Rebelliousness, Insecure, Resentment

My Pre-exercise Notes: _____

_____

_____

_____

_____

The suggested step for Exercise 41 is Step 8.

Exercise 42

Nehemiah 8:9-10

Dealing with Godly Sadness

Neh 8:9-10 - And Nehemiah, who was the governor, and Ezra the priest and scribe, and the Levites who taught the people said to all the people, "This day is holy to the Lord your God; do not mourn or weep." For all the people wept as they heard the words of the Law. Then he said to them, "Go your way. Eat the fat and drink sweet wine and send portions to anyone who has nothing ready, for this day is holy to our Lord. And do not be grieved, for the joy of the Lord is your strength." ESV

Guiding Commentary – The scene is this; the people of Israel had been in exile for close to 150 years (of which 70 years were in captivity) and Nehemiah had been given permission to go back to Jerusalem to rebuild the city. During the reconstruction, scrolls of the Mosaic Law were discovered. When the people, who had forgotten the Law and were not following God's ordinances, heard the Law being read to them they were moved into grief over the losses they had because of their own drifting from God. They wept tears of godly sorrow. Nehemiah, showing amazing leadership and prompted by God, told the Israelites not to grieve with depression, but to throw a party, and celebrate the restoration of the Law into their nation. This is great advice for those of us in recovery. We too drifted from God and His ways, and then we came out of our self-imposed exile and rediscovered God's instructions, and we were grieved at all of our losses. God's instruction through Nehemiah is as valid today as it was then. Yes we can grieve, and we can feel godly remorse. God says to follow this as quickly as possible by celebrating our recovery, our restoration, because the joy of the Lord is our strength!

The Exercise – Write about how you responded to your realization that you had seriously drifted from God and acted out. Did you slip into an understandable depression and stay there for a long time? Were some of those around you full of condemnation or judgment, so much so that you stayed in your grief? Have you come to terms with your acting out and whilst in godly remorse sensed God's forgiveness? Have you celebrated being liberated by God from the natural psychological consequences of your actions?

If you are still stuck in your sorrow, do you find this instruction from God to be encouraging? Are you ready to celebrate with your recovery group friends your freedom from slavery to your acting out? Write out an idea or two on how you might celebrate.

Sponsor Notes: _____

_____

_____

Useful Feeling Words:

- Depressed, Grieving, Ashamed, Joyful, Relieved

Useful Attitudinal Words:

- Fearful, Gratefulness, Resentment, Punishment, Relief

My Pre-exercise Notes: _____

_____

_____

_____

The suggested step for Exercise 42 is Step 4.

Exercise 43

Job 38:2

Sincerely Wrong or Right

Job 38:2 - Who is this that darkens counsel by words without knowledge? ESV

<u>Guiding Commentary</u> – This is God saying to Job, in a very nice way, "Who do you think you are, messing with my plans and my purposes, by speaking from ignorance?"

In recovery we will meet well-intentioned individuals, (and I'm sure I've done this myself), that attempt to help us by telling us what God says about a particular subject or issue in our lives. The problem is that we are often well-intentioned, and sincere, but we are also sincerely wrong. And when we are wrong we are messing with God's plans and purposes in an individual's life.

In the light of this reality the sincere people, like myself and others I work with, must be careful that we don't quench the Spirit (1 Thess 5:19) which I have called "mess with God's plans and purposes." There are three major ways we do this:

1. By misapplying scripture.
2. By giving someone a false "word from the Lord."
3. By making ourselves out to be experts in scripture interpretation when we aren't.

None of this is meant to dissuade a person from helping others; it is merely a call to be careful in how we help. The more we know scripture, the more we communicate with God through prayer and the more we live our lives in humility before God, the more likely we are to avoid the three common mistakes listed above.

<u>The Exercise</u> - Have you ever given advice or counsel to an individual in recovery? Of course you have! In this exercise we are going to look at how we are doing with this.

Start by writing down in detail an example or two, of times you have given counsel to a person in recovery, and although you were sincere, you now realize that you were sincerely wrong.

Now do the same for one or two times you were correct.

Finally can you explain the difference between your "sincerely wrong" and your right times.

Sponsor Notes: _____

_____

_____

Useful Feeling Words:

- Sorry, Guilty, Glad, Disillusioned, Upset

Useful Attitudinal Words:

- Gratefulness, Sorrowfulness, Disturbed, Remorseful, Paranoid

My Pre-exercise Notes: _____

_____

_____

_____

_____

The suggested step for Exercise 43 is Step 12.

Exercise 44

Genesis 3:8

<u>What Shame Does</u>

Gen 3:8 - And they heard the sound of the Lord God walking in the garden in the cool of the day, and the man and his wife hid themselves from the presence of the Lord God among the trees of the garden. *ESV*

<u>Guiding Commentary</u> – This is of course part of the classic story of the fall of mankind; this part is where Adam and Eve get caught in their rebellion and their response is to run away and hide. It is so human to want to hide our sins, we don't want to be exposed, and there is a good reason for this. Earlier in the story (Gen 2:25) the first couple are described as being naked and not ashamed. In the context of recovery we need to understand that before Adam and Eve "acted out" they had no shame. When they acted out and they were about to be exposed they were captured by the fear of exposure and felt the overwhelming power of shame in their lives. As any seasoned recovery veteran will attest to, when we act out with no fear of exposure, we feel no shame. Once we start to recognize our acting out behaviors and become fearful at some level, we start to feel shame. Shame will debilitate us, shame will paralyze us, shame will weaken us and hinder us in all parts of our lives. Shame may be the most powerful emotion that God created.

<u>The Exercise</u> – Have you ever run away and hid? Have you been so afraid of someone finding out about your behaviors that you couldn't function properly? In this exercise we want to look at how you have been affected by shame. Go back to the time when you were "successfully" acting out; that is when you were deep into your immoral behaviors; you were having a "good time", you thought no one knew what you were doing, you believed you were getting away with something, you were seeking you own pleasures and not caring how your actions were affecting others and you had no sense of guilt and shame. Write out your version of your pre-recovery acting out story. Then add your first recollection of some feelings that you had that left you uneasy; there might have been some guilt, shame, fear or perhaps a sense of unworthiness. Write about what was happening at that time. Then move on to the moment of exposure. Were you fearful? Can you identify when shame took over as the most dominant emotion in your life? Write about the circumstances surrounding that.

In the second part of this exercise we want to look at how you managed to finally deal with the shame in your life. Write out how the realization came to you that the power of secret shame was holding you back from confessing to God and others what you had done. As you write, add in a description of how when you first confessed things it was hard, but you felt strangely relieved afterwards. Describe the feeling you had as the burden of your shame was lifted. Do you believe that you were the one that did the heavy lifting? If not, write about the who and what of this shame-lifting event or events. Finally write about how you handle shame today.

Sponsor Notes: _____

_____

_____

Useful Feeling Words:

- Ashamed, Exposed, Confused, Reluctant, Evasive

Useful Attitudinal Words:

- Depression, Fearful, Bitterness, Anxiety, Victimhood

My Pre-exercise Notes: _____

_____

_____

_____

_____

The suggested step for Exercise 44 is Step 4.

Exercise 45

Amos 7:7-8

Addressing Your Plumb Line

Amos 7:7-8 - This is what he showed me: behold, the Lord was standing beside a wall built with a plumb line, with a plumb line in his hand. And the Lord said to me, "Amos, what do you see?" And I said, "A plumb line." Then the Lord said, "Behold, I am setting a plumb line in the midst of my people Israel; I will never again pass by them." ESV

Guiding Commentary – In this scripture we see God illustrate a simple principle. A plumb line is a piece of lead tied to some string which is used to gauge whether something, usually a building, is vertically straight. If the building structure doesn't have straight walls then everything will ultimately bend, break or collapse. The plumb line provides a method of determining the building's integrity. God has said that He is going to put a plumb line in our lives, and He will measure them by it, and he will allow the consequences of our actions to occur. All of us in recovery recognize that has happened to us. The plumb line is God's word, and we have failed to measure up to the standards laid out in it, so we have experienced the consequences of our actions. Our initial response here ought to be one of realization that God's word is supremely authoritative in providing a perfect plumb line for us. The next part of this response ought to be one of heartfelt delight in confessing that we have built the walls of our lives using a faulty plumb line to ourselves, others and God. The final part of our response ought then to be a declaration that we want to stop doing things our way and start doing them His way, using His plumb line.

The Exercise – Take a look back and see what kind of plumb line you were using before recovery and compare it the time after you got sober, and then also compare it to today. Do this by identifying the values, beliefs and attitudes you had in these three parts of your life. An example might be, to examine who you allowed to influence you and your behaviors. Did you believe it was okay to "act out" back then, did you think that simply stopping your behavior (getting sober) was enough? There is no right or wrong in this exercise, we simply want to identify our changing plumb line, and see how through Christian recovery we have finally come around to the understanding that God's word is our plumb line.

Write a prayer of gratitude to God for how He has worked in your life to get you from your personal pit to a place of ongoing victory in your life. Thank Him for the people He has put in your life, thank Him for His Holy Spirit and thank Him for His plumb line, the word of God. In your prayer, be specific about things, naming names of those who have been part of your journey, identifying times the Spirit has spoken to you and record when the word of God has renewed your mind.

Sponsor Notes: _____

_____

_____

Useful Feeling Words:

- Ashamed, Glad, Beaten-down, Aware, Broken

Useful Attitudinal Words:

- Broken-heartedness, Thankfulness, Victimhood, Unbelief, Apathy

My Pre-exercise Notes: _____

_____

_____

_____

_____

The suggested step for Exercise 45 is Step 5.

Exercise 46

Romans 6:5-7

<u>Removing Character Defects</u>

Rom 6:5-7 - For if we have been united with him in a death like his, we shall certainly be united with him in a resurrection like his. We know that our old self was crucified with him in order that the body of sin might be brought to nothing, so that we would no longer be enslaved to sin. For one who has died has been set free from sin. ESV

<u>Guiding Commentary</u> – Deep in the middle of this portion of scripture we find something very profound. It says that our old self has to be crucified, meaning killed off, so that our "body of sin might be done away with". In the context of recovery we can see this quite clearly speaks to the change we must all make. We must kill off our character defects which control our acting out so that they, and the associated behaviors, can be done away with. We have to have God remove our character defects for us, as we cannot do it ourselves, and then our actions will become more godly in nature. If we choose to not let God work in us to remove our character defects we are dooming ourselves to a life of slavery to our sinful lusts and behaviors. This speaks to the recovery principle that we cannot change our character; we must ask God to remove our character defects and replace them with character integrity.

<u>The Exercise</u> – In this exercise we want to take a look at the work we have done or are doing about our character defects. First, write out a summary of some of the major defects (suggested limit of five) you have identified with the help of your sponsor of mentor, remembering that you cannot see yourself as God sees you or as others see you. If you have done a personal moral inventory, these defects ought to be listed there. As you list these defects, also document at least one acting out event that resulted from each one. This helps us link character defects to behavior. Then record if you believe that the listed defect has been removed or not. If you genuinely believe the defect is removed, identify what has replaced it, and write out a short prayer of thanks to God.

If you are still struggling with some character defects, write out a prayer of petition to God to have them removed. And finally, write down your thoughts on why God may choose to not remove them until a time He will determine. In this last part of the exercise, pay particular attention to the idea of your internal willingness, and any other relevant attitudes, to live in obedience to God.

Sponsor Notes: _____

_____

_____

Useful Feeling Words:

- Ashamed, Ready, Confused, Scarred, Wounded

Useful Attitudinal Words:

- Overwhelming, Gratefulness, Expectant, Hopefulness, Confident

My Pre-exercise Notes: _____

_____

_____

_____

_____

The suggested step for Exercise 46 is Step 6.

Exercise 47

1 Timothy 4:14-16

<u>Don't Neglect Your Gift</u>

1 Tim 4:14-16 - Do not neglect the gift you have, which was given you by prophecy when the council of elders laid their hands on you. Practice these things, devote yourself to them, so that all may see your progress. Keep a close watch on yourself and on the teaching. Persist in this, for by so doing you will save both yourself and your hearers. ESV

<u>Guiding Commentary</u> – The journey of recovery is always characterized by certain spiritual markers. One of them is listed here; it is called a spiritual gift. Even though each of us may choose to stay in recovery groups or fellowships there is a point at which we realize that we have achieved much. In the 12 step world, it is called the twelfth step. This doesn't represent an end of our journey, it is better thought of as a change in our journey. At this time we realize that we have been given much by God and we are characterized by our thankfulness and willingness to give back or serve. Each of us has been enabled by God in some way to take all that we have learned and experienced, and use it to help others. We may lead groups, serve coffee at meetings, or do other service activities. The most important thing we do though is to share our story. Our focus scripture identifies that this helps to ensure salvation for others. In recovery, we know we cannot save others ourselves, and we also know that we have a responsibility to do our part, and that God will use us to help others. We must not neglect to use our gifts, because each time we do use it, we are glorifying God.

<u>The Exercise</u> – Our scripture says to pay close attention to ourselves. Write about the ways you are using the gift of your story to help others in recovery. Are you serving as an organizer or a sponsor or in some other way? Do you "witness", meaning tell your story, to others when appropriate? Also write out how this helps (or not) you in maintaining your sobriety or in other ways in recovery.

If you have chosen to not serve the general fellowship of recovery in some way, write out why you have made this choice. Look at any barriers you might have to "giving back". Are there fears still lingering inside? Are there any other emotional or attitudinal barriers? Do you have a spouse or other family member who is getting in the way somehow? Don't blame them for this, but explain how they might be interfering with your desire and duty to give back. Examine your level of gratefulness; does it lead you to want to give back?

Finally write out any personal thoughts you might have on the subject of receiving and using gifts from God in recovery.

Sponsor Notes: _____

_____

_____

Useful Feeling Words:

- Grateful, Happy, Blessed, Honored, Ready

Useful Attitudinal Words:

- Thankfulness, Cheerfulness, Readiness, Servant-heartedness, Activated

My Pre-exercise Notes: _____

_____

_____

_____

_____

The suggested step for Exercise 47 is Step 12.

Exercise 48

James 1:23-25

Work the Program

James 1:23-25 - For if anyone is a hearer of the word and not a doer, he is like a man who looks intently at his natural face in a mirror. For he looks at himself and goes away and at once forgets what he was like. But the one who looks into the perfect law, the law of liberty, and perseveres, being no hearer who forgets but a doer who acts, he will be blessed in his doing. ESV

Guiding Commentary – "Working the program" is a term very familiar to people in recovery. It refers to the idea that a person must be diligent in putting personal effort into moving through the 12 steps or other recovery system. Not "working the program" almost always leads to failure or very limited success in overcoming compulsions or addictions. In our scripture we see God saying this in His own unique way. He says don't just hear the word, but do what it says, meaning don't just listen to sermons and read the Bible or other god-centered books, do what God tells you to do. It then says we are to be "doers who act" meaning live out the teachings of scripture, and not be a forgetful hearer but an effectual doer, because then we will be blessed. It is the same in recovery; don't just go to meetings and listen and read the books, but actually do what we are told will work. This is where recovery success lies; it is the doing that leads to healing. God will always do His part, and we must be "doers" of our part.

The Exercise – Are you a mere hearer of recovery words, not putting into practice what you are hearing? The chances are that if you doing this exercise you have been a "doer" and God is blessing you and as a result you are achieving success. You are to be commended for being diligent in "working the program."

In this exercise we are to take a look at ourselves and make a self-assessment at estimating our level of diligence in "working our program". Without consulting anybody for help, write out a list of the things you have heard that you need to do, and then check this list to see if you have been doing them. For example you may have been told to write out you fourth step 30 minutes each day, and you haven't been doing it. In doing this exercise you may have to gather up some of the materials you have collected in recovery to be able to recollect what you have been told ought to be done to work the program.

Once you have completed reviewing the material and doing an introspective look at yourself write out a one paragraph statement on your recovery performance in "working the program" as if you were doing an employee performance appraisal. Give yourself an honest grade, and then discuss this appraisal with your sponsor or mentor.

Sponsor Notes: _____

_____

_____

Useful Feeling Words:

- Lethargic, Lazy, Confident, Blessed, Happy

Useful Attitudinal Words:

- Laziness, Rebelliousness, Hard-hearted, Avoidance, Perseverance

My Pre-exercise Notes: _____

_____

_____

_____

_____

The suggested step for Exercise 48 is Step 10.

Exercise 49

Mark 10:13-15

Childlike Powerlessness

Mark 10:13-15 - And they were bringing children to him that he might touch them, and the disciples rebuked them. But when Jesus saw it, he was indignant and said to them, "Let the children come to me; do not hinder them, for to such belongs the kingdom of God. Truly, I say to you, whoever does not receive the kingdom of God like a child shall not enter it." ESV

Guiding Commentary – The disciples were preventing people from bringing their children to Jesus, and Jesus used that opportunity to correct the thinking of His disciples and teach us a very important spiritual principle. Children are powerless; they rely on their earthly mothers and fathers for everything. We are powerless, and before recovery we didn't know that. Jesus is speaking a small sentence with life changing meaning. He is explaining to all who will listen that we must have a childlike powerlessness to be able to receive the kingdom of God. In the context of recovery this means that to move into God's healing for us, whatever form that takes, we must acknowledge the truth that we are powerless. This is why so many recovery programs, including secular programs, start with admitting powerlessness. It is a spiritual principle and it cannot be violated because if it wasn't true it would make God a liar. He said that He is the healer (Ex 15:26), which means that no one else is, and that we are powerless over our compulsions, addictions and diseases. To enter into His healing we must recognize like a child, that we are powerless.

The Exercise – Go back to the time when you entered into recovery. Do you agree that you had to admit powerlessness over your "ism" before you could begin to heal? Or, were you one of those that only admitted powerlessness over a small portion of your life? Were you childlike in your attitudes toward moving into recovery? Write out a description of your psychological condition as you began your time in recovery, paying particular attention to how you dealt with lingering doubts about God's ability to help you, as well as rebellious or disobedient attitudes. Include information about how you thought about recovery at that time, and also include descriptions of your impulsive behaviors during the time you finally came to realize that you were powerless.

Finally, write out a list of the things you are still holding onto, things that you continue to believe you have power and control over. Write out a prayer of request to God for His help in moving you from holding on to these things to admitting you are powerless over them. Include a plea for Him to help you by relieving you of the burdens you are carrying because you believe you have power and control. Ask Him to help you become fully childlike in your attitudes about what you think you control.

Sponsor Notes: _____

_____

_____

Useful Feeling Words:

- Impotent, Powerless, Rebellious, Wrong, Strong

Useful Attitudinal Words:

- Rebelliousness, Disobedient, Resentment, Arrogant, Quarrelsome

My Pre-exercise Notes: _____

_____

_____

_____

_____

The suggested step for Exercise 49 is Step 1.

Exercise 50

Matthew 7:6

<u>Be Aware of Unsafe People</u>

Matt 7:6 - Do not give dogs what is holy, and do not throw your pearls before pigs, lest they trample them underfoot and turn to attack you. ESV

<u>Guiding Commentary</u> – The sequence of words here can be confusing. It is the dogs who will turn and tear us to pieces and the pigs that will trample our pearls into the ground. Dogs and pigs were unclean animals to the Jewish people, and in most of the Middle East they still are. Jesus is speaking here and telling us not to give what we have already given to God to the wrong people (dogs) and not to hand over any precious things we have to wrong people (pigs). This has great application in recovery. When we come to Christ for His help, we give our stories and our recovery program over to Him, we make them holy, set aside in honor of Him. Christ warns us in this verse that if we give (share) these things to unsafe people they will turn on us and emotionally tear us up. He also tells us to not give or share our valuable achievements in recovery with unsafe people as they will try to crush our souls, by denying their value in our lives and demeaning us in some way. This is a good warning to us in recovery!

<u>The Exercise</u> – Write about your negative experiences of sharing your recovery situation or story with others. Identify who you shared with and what you shared where they responded in some of the following ways. Did they dismiss or minimize you and your efforts; did they gossip about you, breaking the confidential nature of your story; did they bring it back up later and use your recovery against you; were you not believed by some; did some of the dogs and pigs try to shame you; did you go through any emotional trauma as a result of their reactions?

As a result of these experiences are you more careful about how you approach others? Write about how you identify and handle unsafe people. What do you do to protect your holy things and your pearls?

Sponsor Notes: _____

_____

_____

Useful Feeling Words:

- Careful, Hurt, Disrespected, Disgusted, Paranoid

Useful Attitudinal Words:

- Cynical, Disdainful, Distrusting, Vexed, Incredulous

My Pre-exercise Notes: _____

_____

_____

_____

_____

The suggested step for Exercise 50 is Step 12.

Addendum 1

Exercises by Suggested Step

No.	Scripture	Theme	Step	Page
1	Rom 7:14-20	Understanding Myself	1	4
25	2 Cor 7:10	Godly or Worldly Sorrow	1	52
30	1 Kings 5:1-15	Responding to Powerlessness	1	62
49	Mark 10:13-15	Childlike Powerlessness	1	100
19	Ezek 36:25-27	Getting a Heart of Flesh	2	40
2	Rom 7:21-25	Internal Conflict	3	6
12	Col 2:8	Don't Be Fooled	3	26
23	Jn 5:5-6	Wanting to be Healed	3	48
26	Mt 6:25a-33	Solving Anxiety	3	54
28	Jonah 2:8-9	Making a New Vow	3	58
34	Mic 6:8	Will of God	3	70
37	Dt 8:5-6	The Lord Disciplines	3	76
40	2 Sam 9:6-7	From Defeat to Restoration	3	82
10	Mark 12:28-31	Loving Oneself	4	22
13	Lam 3:40-41	Looking Inside	4	28
21	Jas 1:19-21	Moral Filth and Anger	4	44
27	Jn 3:19-21	Light or Darkness	4	56
31	Rom 1:18-20	God is Evident - No Excuses	4	64
42	Neh 8:9-10	Dealing with Godly Sadness	4	86
44	Gen 3:8	What Shame Does	4	90
7	Jas 5:16	Confession to One Another	5	16
8	1 Jn 1:8-10	Confession to God	5	18
45	Amos 7:7-8	Addressing Your Plumb Line	5	92
6	2 Cor 3:16-17	Out of Captivity	6	14
15	Luke 14:11	Humility is Necessary	6	32

Addendum 2

Exercises by Scripture Reference

No.	Scripture	Theme	Step	Page
18	1 Cor 10:13	Dealing With Temptations	10	38
20	1 Cor 15:33	Keeping Good Company	6	42
8	1 Jn 1:8-10	Confession to God	5	18
30	1 Kings 5:1-15	Responding to Powerlessness	1	62
36	1 Sam 12:20-23	Your Part - His Promise	11	74
14	1 Sam 15:22-23(a)	Obedience or Rebellion	11	30
47	1 Tim 4:14-16	Don't Neglect Your Gift	12	96
11	2 Cor 1:3-4	Comforting Others	12	24
17	2 Cor 10:5	Capturing our Thoughts	10	36
6	2 Cor 3:16-17	Out of Captivity	6	14
25	2 Cor 7:10	Godly or Worldly Sorrow	1	52
40	2 Sam 9:6-7	From Defeat to Restoration	3	82
41	Acts 19:18	Full Disclosure	8	84
45	Amos 7:7-8	Addressing Your Plumb Line	5	92
12	Col 2:8	Don't Be Fooled	3	26
37	Dt 8:5-6	The Lord Disciplines	3	76
29	Eph 4:22-24	Putting on a New Self	6	60
16	Eph 4:25	Speaking Truth	9	34
3	Eph 6:16	How is Your Shield?	10	8
39	Ex 22:9	Payment of Restitution	8	80
19	Ezek 36:25-27	Getting a Heart of Flesh	2	40
22	Gal 6:1-2	Being Thankful For Others	12	46
33	Gal 6:7-10	Sowing and Reaping	8	68
44	Gen 3:8	What Shame Does	4	90
21	Jas 1:19-21	Moral Filth and Anger	4	44

48	Jas 1:23-25	Work the Program	10	98
7	Jas 5:16	Confession to One Another	5	16
4	Jn 1:14	Truth or Grace?	12	10
27	Jn 3:19-21	Light or Darkness	4	56
23	Jn 5:5-6	Wanting to be Healed	3	48
32	Jn 8:10-11	Go and Sin No More	7	66
43	Job 38:2	Sincerely Wrong or Right?	12	88
28	Jonah 2:8-9	Making a New Vow	3	58
24	Judg 2:11-12	Don't Turn Back	7	50
13	Lam 3:40-41	Looking Inside	4	28
15	Luke 14:11	Humility is Necessary	6	32
49	Mark 10:13-15	Childlike Powerlessness	1	100
10	Mark 12:28-31	Loving Oneself	4	22
34	Mic 6:8	Will of God	3	70
38	Mt 6:19-21	Eternal Treasures	12	78
26	Mt 6:25a-33	Solving Anxiety	3	54
50	Mt 7:6	Be Aware of Unsafe People	12	102
42	Neh 8:9-10	Dealing with Godly Sadness	4	86
5	Phil 2:12-13	Cleansing of the Heart	10	12
31	Rom 1:18-20	God is Evident - No Excuses	4	64
9	Rom 12:1-2	Transformation	7	20
46	Rom 6:5-7	Removing Character Defects	6	94
1	Rom 7:14-20	Understanding Myself	1	4
2	Rom 7:21-25	Internal Conflict	3	6
35	Zeph 3:17	When God Rejoices	11	72

Addendum 3

List of Feeling and Attitude Words

Positive Tone/Attitude/Emotion Words

Amiable	Consoling	Friendly	Playful
Amused	Content	Happy	Pleasant
Appreciative	Dreamy	Hopeful	Proud
Authoritative	Ecstatic	Impassioned	Relaxed
Benevolent	Elated	Jovial	Reverent
Brave	Elevated	Joyful	Romantic
Calm	Encouraging	Jubilant	Soothing
Cheerful	Energetic	Lighthearted	Surprised
Cheery	Enthusiastic	Loving	Sweet
Compassionate	Excited	Optimistic	Sympathetic
Complimentary	Exuberant	Passionate	Vibrant
Confident	Fanciful	Peaceful	Whimsical

Negative Tone/Attitude/Emotion Words

Accusing	Choleric	Furious	Quarrelsome
Aggravated	Coarse	Harsh	Shameful
Agitated	Cold	Haughty	Smooth
Angry	Condemnatory	Hateful	Snooty
Apathetic	Condescending	Hurtful	Superficial
Arrogant	Contradictory	Indignant	Surly
Artificial	Critical	Inflammatory	Testy
Audacious	Desperate	Insulting	Threatening
Belligerent	Disappointed	Irritated	Tired
Bitter	Disgruntled	Manipulative	Uninterested
Boring	Disgusted	Obnoxious	Wrathful
Brash	Disinterested	Outraged	
Childish	Facetious	Passive	

Humor-Irony-Sarcasm Tone/Attitude/Emotion Words

Amused	Droll	Mock-heroic	Sardonic
Bantering	Facetious	Mocking	Satiric
Bitter	Flippant	Mock-serious	Scornful
Caustic	Giddy	Patronizing	Sharp
Comical	Humorous	Pompous	Silly
Condescending	Insolent	Quizzical	Taunting
Contemptuous	Ironic	Ribald	Teasing
Critical	Irreverent	Ridiculing	Whimsical
Cynical	Joking	Sad	Wry
Disdainful	Malicious	Sarcastic	

Sorrow-Fear-Worry Tone/Attitude/Emotion Words

Aggravated	Embarrassed	Morose	Resigned
Agitated	Fearful	Mournful	Sad
Anxious	Foreboding	Nervous	Serious
Apologetic	Gloomy	Numb	Sober
Apprehensive	Grave	Ominous	Solemn
Concerned	Hollow	Paranoid	Somber
Confused	Hopeless	Pessimistic	Staid
Dejected	Horrific	Pitiful	Upset
Depressed	Horror	Poignant	
Despairing	Melancholy	Regretful	
Disturbed	Miserable	Remorseful	

Neutral Tone/Attitude/Emotion Words

Admonitory	Dramatic	Intimate	Questioning
Allusive	Earnest	Judgmental	Reflective
Apathetic	Expectant	Learned	Reminiscent
Authoritative	Factual	Loud	Resigned
Baffled	Fervent	Lyrical	Restrained
Callous	Formal	Matter-of-fact	Seductive
Candid	Forthright	Meditative	Sentimental
Ceremonial	Frivolous	Nostalgic	Serious
Clinical	Haughty	Objective	Shocking
Consoling	Histrionic	Obsequious	Sincere
Contemplative	Humble	Patriotic	Unemotional
Conventional	Incredulous	Persuasive	Urgent
Detached	Informative	Pleading	Vexed
Didactic	Inquisitive	Pretentious	Wistful
Disbelieving	Instructive	Provocative	Zealous

This organized list is provided to help those who are working on the exercises in these books. Emotion and attitude words are very useful in helping prepare answers to questions and for mentors, sponsors, coaches and counselors in their work with those in recovery.

Addendum 4

Ten Emotional Needs

During our time in recovery we have noticed time and again a common theme running through the stories we hear. There seem to be some emotional needs that we all have in common and that are so often glaringly not met in those who live a life involving significant compulsive behaviors. This list is provided for sponsors, mentors, counselors or other spiritual guides and the individuals who use this book as an aide in working through issues. As a person works a program or walks through counseling, this list might help unlock some things for them.

These are listed in alphabetical order; different individuals need different amounts of these, and/or have different levels of deficits of these in their life.

- **Acceptance** - deliberate and ready reception with favorable positive response (Rom. 15:7)
- **Affection** - to communicate care and closeness through physical touch (Rom. 16:16)
- **Appreciation** - to communicate with words and feelings a personal gratefulness for another (1 Cor. 11:2)
- **Approval** - to think and speak well of (Rom. 14:18)
- **Attention** - to take thought of another and convey interest and support; to enter into another's world (I Cor. 12:25)
- **Comfort (empathy)** - to come alongside with word, feeling, and touch; to give consolation with tenderness (Rom. 12:15)
- **Encouragement** - to urge forward and positively persuade toward a goal (I Thess. 5:11, Heb. 10:24)
- **Respect** - to value and regard highly; to convey great worth (Phil. 2:4)
- **Security** - confidence of harmony in relationships; free from harm (Rom. 12:16a)
- **Support** - come alongside and gently help carry a load (Gal. 6:2)

Addendum 5

Exercise Record

Use this simple log sheet to keep a record of when you did an exercise and any quick thought you may have about it for your own future reference. It has been helpful to some to go back and do an exercise again a few months after doing it for the first time and comparing their answers.

	Exercise Theme	Date	Short Comment
1	Understanding Myself		
2	Internal Conflict		
3	How is Your Shield?		
4	Truth or Grace?		
5	Cleansing of the Heart		
6	Out of Captivity		
7	Confession to One Another		
8	Confession to God		
9	Transformation		
10	Loving Oneself		
11	Comforting Others		
12	Don't Be Fooled		
13	Looking Inside		
14	Obedience or Rebellion		
15	Humility is Necessary		
16	Speaking Truth		
17	Capturing our Thoughts		
18	Dealing With Temptations		
19	Getting a Heart of Flesh		
20	Keeping Good Company		
21	Moral Filth and Anger		
22	Being Thankful For Others		
23	Wanting to be Healed		

24	Don't Turn Back	_____	_____
25	Godly or Worldly Sorrow	_____	_____
26	Solving Anxiety	_____	_____
27	Light or Darkness	_____	_____
28	Making a New Vow	_____	_____
29	Putting on a New Self	_____	_____
30	Responding to Powerlessness	_____	_____
31	God is Evident - No Excuses	_____	_____
32	Go and Sin No More	_____	_____
33	Sowing and Reaping	_____	_____
34	Will of God	_____	_____
35	When God Rejoices	_____	_____
36	Your Part - His Promise	_____	_____
37	The Lord Disciplines	_____	_____
38	Eternal Treasures	_____	_____
39	Payment of Restitution	_____	_____
40	From Defeat to Restoration	_____	_____
41	Full Disclosure	_____	_____
42	Dealing with Godly Sadness	_____	_____
43	Sincerely Wrong or Right?	_____	_____
44	What Shame Does	_____	_____
45	Addressing Your Plumb Line	_____	_____
46	Removing Character Defects	_____	_____
47	Don't Neglect Your Gift	_____	_____
48	Work the Program	_____	_____
49	Childlike Powerlessness	_____	_____
50	Be Aware of Unsafe People	_____	_____

Addendum 6 - Example 12 Steps

This is a list of the 12 steps for one of Merimnao's support groups, used by permission of Merimnao Healing Ministry. This particular list is from their Castimonia – Men's Sexual Purity Group, see Castimonia.org for information on them and how to contact the group.

1. **We admitted we were powerless over our addictions and compulsive behaviors, that our lives had become unmanageable.** *"I know that nothing good lives in me, that is, in my sinful nature. For I have the desire to do what is good, but I cannot carry it out."* (Romans 7:18)

2. **We came to believe that a power greater than ourselves could restore us to sanity.** *"For it is God who works in you to will and to act according to his good purpose."* (Philippians 2:13)

3. **We made a decision to turn our lives and our wills over to the care of God.** *"Humble yourselves, therefore, under God's mighty hand, that he may lift you up in due time. Cast all your anxiety on Him because He cares for you."* (1 Peter 5:6-7)

4. **We made a searching and fearless moral inventory of ourselves.** *"Let us examine our ways and test them, and let us return to the LORD."* (Lamentations 3:40)

5. **We admitted to God, to ourselves, and to another human being the exact nature of our wrongs.** *"Therefore confess your sins to each other and pray for each other so that you may be healed."* (James 5:16)

6. **We were entirely ready to have God remove all these defects of character.** *"Humble yourselves before the Lord, and he will lift you up."* (James 4:10)

7. **We humbly ask Him to remove all our shortcomings.** *"If we confess our sins, he is faithful and just and will forgive us our sins and purify us from all unrighteousness."* (1 John 1:9)

8. **We made a list of all persons we had harmed and became willing to make amends to them all.** *"Be kind and compassionate to one another, forgiving each other, just as in Christ, God forgave you."* (Ephesians 4:32)

9. **We made direct amends to such people whenever possible, except when to do so would injure them or others.** *"*Be devoted to one another in brotherly love. Honor one another above yourselves. If it is possible, as far as it depends on you, live at peace with everyone.*"* (Romans 12:10, 18)

10. **We continued to take personal inventory and when we were wrong, promptly admitted it.** *"So, if you think you are standing firm, be careful that you don't fall!"* (1 Corinthians 10:12)

11. **We sought through prayer and meditation to improve our conscious contact with God, praying only for knowledge of His will for us and the power to carry that out.** *"Do not conform any longer to the pattern of this world, but be transformed by the renewing of your mind. Then you will be able to test and approve what God's will is – His good, pleasing, and perfect will."* (Romans 12:2)

12. **Having had a spiritual experience as the result of these steps, we try to carry this message to others and to practice these principles in all our affairs.** *"Praise be to the God and Father of our Lord Jesus Christ, the Father of compassion and the God of all comfort, who comforts us in all our troubles, so that we can comfort those in any trouble with the comfort we ourselves have received from God."* (2 Corinthians 1:3-4)

Addendum 7

The Three Books

There are three books in this series "Recovery Exercises for Christians" each having 50 written exercises for those in the world of Christian recovery to use.

1. Random Scriptures
2. Books of Wisdom
3. Characters of the Bible

Random Scriptures is a set of exercises that are taken from all over the Bible. Books of Wisdom is 50 exercises taken out of the three books of wisdom, Psalms, Proverbs and Ecclesiastes. Characters of the Bible is a set of 50 exercises based on the lives of real people as described in scripture.

The development of the three books occurred as we worked with sponsees on the early part of their programs, and noticed that there was a need for some scripture-centered study material. This came out of some core beliefs we have. First, that scripture is the infallible source for all written wisdom, given to us by God Himself for use as a guide to real life. Second, that the Bible itself is the book of recovery; it contains the story of God's work to recover the entire human race. This makes our God the God of recovery.

It is our contention that all peoples in all nations ought to consider themselves in recovery, because we believe this is true:

Rom 3:23 - For all have sinned and fall short of the glory of God. ESV

Every human has fallen short, and all need to be recovered. We hope that these three books contribute to that happening in some people's lives.

My Notes

Use the next few pages to write out your random thoughts, individual musings, deep meditations or personal revelations. Be sure to date them for your records.

My Notes - Page 2

My Notes - Page 3

My Notes - Page 4

www.ingramcontent.com/pod-product-compliance
Lightning Source LLC
Chambersburg PA
CBHW080415290526
45791CB00008BA/2285